LAW, PSYCHIATRY
and the
MENTALLY DISORDERED
OFFENDER

LAW, PSYCHIATRY
and the
MENTALLY DISORDERED
OFFENDER
Volume II

Edited by

LYNN M. IRVINE, JR., C.S.W., A.C.S.W.

Mental Health Administrator
Department of Mental Health
Illinois Security Hospital
Chester, Illinois

and

TERRY B. BRELJE, Ph.D.

Administrator
Department of Corrections
Psychiatric Division
Menard, Illinois

CHARLES C THOMAS • PUBLISHER

Springfield • Illinois • U.S.A.

Published and Distributed Throughout the World by
CHARLES C THOMAS • PUBLISHER
BANNERSTONE HOUSE
301-327 East Lawrence Avenue, Springfield, Illinois, U.S.A.

© 1973, by CHARLES C THOMAS • PUBLISHER
ISBN 0-398-02645-9
Library of Congress Catalog Card Number: 72 75921

With THOMAS BOOKS *careful attention is given to all details of*
manufacturing and design. It is the Publisher's desire to present books
that are satisfactory as to their physical qualities and artistic possibilities
and appropriate for their particular use. THOMAS BOOKS *will be true*
to those laws of quality that assure a good name and good will.

Proceedings of an Institute held at
Southern Illinois University, Carbondale, Illinois

Printed in the United States of America
JJ-23

To

The Mentally Disordered Offender

CONTRIBUTORS

NORMAN I. BARR, M.D.

Coordinator of Clinical Services
Institute for Reality Therapy
Los Angeles, California

JOHN BURCHARD, Ph.D.

Acting Director
Clinical Training Program
Psychology Department
University of Vermont
Burlington, Vermont

THOMAS G. EYNON, Ph.D.

Professor
Center for the Study of Crime, Delinquency, and Corrections
Southern Illinois University
Carbondale, Illinois

MAXWELL JONES, M.D.

Senior Consultant
Staff Development
Fort Logan Mental Health Center
Denver, Colorado

JOSEPH S. LOBENTHAL, JR., J.D.

Lawyer and Legal Consultant
Faculty, The New School of Social Research
New York, New York

GUY MERSEREAU, M.D.

Director
Forensic Psychiatry Service
Erie County Department of Mental Health
Buffalo, New York

SENECA H. NOLAN, JR., J.D.

Legal Adviser
Metropolitan Police Department, City of St. Louis
St. Louis, Missouri

ROBERT E. SCHULMAN, J.D., Ph.D.

Clinical Psychologist
Division of Law and Psychiatry
Menninger Clinic
Topeka, Kansas
Associate Professor of Law
University of Kansas
School of Law
Lawrence, Kansas

THOMAS SZASZ, M.D.

Professor of Psychiatry
College of Medicine
Department of Psychiatry
State University Hospital of the
Upstate Medical Center
Syracuse, New York

MARGARET WEEKS, R.N., M.S.

Program Director for Consultation
Staff Development
Fort Logan Mental Health Center
Denver, Colorado

ALBERT WEISSMAN, Ph.D.

Manager
Psychopharmacology
Pfizer Pharmaceuticals
Groton, Connecticut

LEONARD ZUNIN, M.D.

Director
Institute for Reality Therapy
Los Angeles, California

It is not the critic who counts; not the one who points out how the strong man stumbled or where the doer of deeds could have done them better. The credit belongs to the man who is actually in the arena, whose face is marred by dust, sweat, and blood, who strives valiantly with great enthusiasm and devotion. His place shall never be with the cold and timid souls who know neither defeat nor victory.

THEODORE ROOSEVELT

INTRODUCTION

The editors had the privilege of being part of an active effort to upgrade the treatment programs for the mentally disordered offender in the State of Illinois. During that process, it became apparent that there was very little data available on which to rely. In an attempt to alleviate this situation, the editors began formulating plans to bring together a large number of individuals who were similarly involved. The yearly Institute on Law, Psychiatry, and the Mentally Disordered Offender was the result of that effort. It is our hope that the papers contained in these volumes will be beneficial in all efforts to provide more effective, responsible, and humane care and treatment for the mentally disordered offender.

ACKNOWLEDGMENTS

Many were involved in the planning, organization, and operation of the Institute. The following people are given special recognition for their encouragement, assistance, and support:

Clerical Assistants

Rosemary Mahan
Bonnie Phillips
Betty Wagner

Foundation

W. Clement and Jessie V. Stone Foundation

Individuals

Ralph H. Albers
Robert Andreson
Everett R. Beck
Martha E. Brelje
Matthew T. Brelje
Terry Carlton
Judson Childs
J. T. Clark
Michael R. Clowers
Joni Hall
Patricia Hawkins
Ralph W. Hay
Alice W. Irvine
Jane W. Irvine
Sally G. Irvine

David L. Jewell
Donald Karnuth
J. Michael Kelsey
William D. Lodge
Rosemary Mahan
Bonnie Phillips
Martha Roberts
Albert F. Scheckenbach
Earl J. Schnoeker
Yvonne Snyder
Jack Thomas
Vernon J. Uffelman
Richard Vasquez
Betty Wagner

Pharmaceutical Houses

Geigy Pharmaceuticals

Hoffman-LaRoche Incorporated

Pfizer Pharmaceuticals
Pfizer Laboratories Division
J. B. Roerig Division
Sandoz Pharmaceuticals

Schering Corporation

Publishers

Charles C Thomas, Publisher
John Wiley & Sons, Inc., Publishers
Simon & Schuster, Inc.
The University of Chicago Press
The University of Michigan Press

University

Division of Continuing Education
Southern Illinois University at Carbondale
Andrew H. Marcec
Carole Vogt

L.M.I.
T.B.B.

CONTENTS

                                                                    Page

Contributors vii

Introduction xi

Acknowledgments xiii

Chapter

  1. THE MENTALLY DISORDERED OFFENDER—*Thomas G. Eynon* .. 3

  2. JUSTICE IN THE THERAPEUTIC STATE—*Thomas S. Szasz* 18

  3. THE LAW ENFORCEMENT OFFICER AND THE MENTALLY
      DISORDERED OFFENDER—*Seneca H. Nolan, Jr.* 28

  4. DETERMINATION OF COMPETENCY—BURIAL AT THE
      CROSSROAD—*Robert E. Schulman* 37

  5. A LAWYER VIEWS MENTAL HEALTH PERSONNEL—
      Joseph S. Lobenthal, Jr. 51

  6. SYSTEMS APPROACH TO A CORRECTIONAL INSTITUTION—
      Maxwell Jones and Margaret Weeks 73

  7. CAMPUS PRISONS, COMMUNITY PRISONS, AND JUDICIAL
      ADMINISTRATION—*Norman I. Barr and Leonard Zunin* ... 82

  8. CURRENT RESEARCH IN DRUGS AND BEHAVIOR AS IT RELATES
      TO THE MENTALLY DISORDERED OFFENDER—
      Albert Weissman 94

  9. THERAPEUTIC COMMUNITY PRINCIPLES—*Maxwell Jones* 102

 10. BEHAVIOR MODIFICATION WITH THE DELINQUENT
      OFFENDER—*John Burchard* 111

 11. THE TALKING CRIMINAL: A BIOLOGICAL AND POLITICAL
      PHENOMENON—*Guy Mersereau* 120

Index 127

LAW, PSYCHIATRY
and the
MENTALLY DISORDERED
OFFENDER

Chapter 1

THE MENTALLY DISORDERED OFFENDER

Thomas G. Eynon

The term "mentally disordered offender" is widely used. However, what specifically is meant by the term, to whom it applies, what differences exist between states and countries, and other factual and empirical data have not been routinely available. In his paper, Dr. Thomas Eynon presents an integrated and comprehensive review of the literature concerned with the mentally disordered offender. Experimental, as well as descriptive data and summaries are presented. His paper should provide a basic reference for students and professionals working with the mentally disordered offender.

EDITORS

The mentally disordered offender is a social role and when people are so labeled, then others expect them to behave in nonrational ways. Whatever the reasons for loss of control or manifestation of symptoms, being considered mentally ill by others puts a person into a role position. Thomas Scheff (1963) said that many persons take on a stereotyped role of insanity once someone has suggested they are mentally ill. He believes that large numbers of people deviate from social norms without receiving any particular label. However, if this nonconformity is challenged and labeled mental illness by others, the disturbed individual lets himself go and behaves according to a stereotyped notion of mental illness. Substantial numbers of people become mentally ill by being so labeled, and it appears that calling a person mentally ill frequently intensifies his symptoms. The social and personal consequences of being mentally ill are different from the consequences of physical illness. We deal with the expectation that once people are labeled mentally ill, then they are no longer expected to behave responsibly. All societies place a high value on an individual's ability to control his behavior, even his thoughts. In mental illness, a person apparently loses self-control at least from socially significant observers' points of view. This poses a problem for society and, indeed, creates a persistent problem for the person so designated. We might agree with Szasz (1960) that mental illness has been a convenient myth which has outlived whatever usefulness it might have had, or we might agree with Abrahamsen (1944) that all social deviants are insane. Whichever course we choose, the concepts underlying diagnosis of mental disorder merge with the definitions we use for nonconformity to norms.

Elizabeth Casper (1965) asked an interesting question: "If crime and mental illness are forms of culturally derived deviant behavior, then what of the mentally ill criminal?" Sociologists have been concerned with mental illness, with crime, or with both, as specific manifestations of deviant behavior in general. The combination of the two forms of deviant behavior in an individual designated criminally insane has been virtually ignored.

The dearth of information on the mentally disordered offender is a reflection of current societal attitudes. Social and behavioral scientists, as well as laymen, are confused when a person is designated both a criminal and mentally ill. If an individual is mentally ill, he is not considered socially responsible for his criminal behavior. If he is a criminal, however, he is responsible. The idea of a mentally ill criminal is a basic contradiction in terms. Perhaps, it is more meaningful to consider a person just mentally ill, with one symptom of his illness being an illegal act. Specifics on the genesis of mentally ill criminals must be sought in studies of mental illness rather than studies of criminality. For want of a better solution to this philosophical dilemma, we use the term "mentally disordered offender," thus escaping the extremity of illness and criminality.

Robert L. Sadoff (1971) stated that criminal behavior obscures mental illness and the legal structure is used for such purposes. Lawyers also use the psychiatrist to solve legal problems (Lobenthal, 1970). It is imperative that we learn to recognize this so that proper dispositions will be made.

Looking at the mentally disordered offender from another perspective, we question the relationship of mental disorder to crime itself. Bromberg and Thompson (1937) report on a study of about ten thousand prisoners conducted by the psychiatric clinic of the Court of General Sessions (New York) from 1932 to 1936. They indicate that 82 percent of the prisoners were normal. A review of 11 studies of psychiatric evaluations of offenders by Brodsky (1972) indicated that the majority of offenders were normal or had only mild personality defects. Although some experts claim there are many mentally ill individuals in prisons, it also has been asserted by Bluestone (1965) that the number of schizophrenic prison inmates has never been accurately established. Cook (1960) reported that the diagnosis of psychoneurotic or psychotic disorders among inmates at the U. S. Disciplinary Barracks, Leavenworth, Kansas, from 1942 to 1956, was at the 2 percent level.

A survey (Scheidemandel and Kanno, 1969) of 90 facilities for the mentally ill revealed that there were 19,000 admissions of mentally disordered offenders in 1967. Comparing this figure with the total number of patients admitted to public mental hospitals (350,000) in 1967, we see that mentally disordered offender admissions constitute about 5 percent of all admissions to the 90 mental hospitals. Comparing mentally disordered offender admissions with the total number of admissions in 1967 to state penal institutions, we find they represented about 16 percent of the 116,432 admissions (Federal Bureau of Prisons, 1969).

For clarification at this point, it may be useful to conceptualize the mentally disordered offender as falling into one of six possible categories. These categories are listed below and are followed by a review of the literature.

1. Persons held pending determination of their competency to stand trial (about 40 percent).
2. Persons transferred from penal institutions who became mentally ill while serving sentences (about 20 percent).
3. Persons charged with a crime who have been found incompetent to stand trial (about 15 percent).
4. Sex offenders not included in other categories (about 15 percent).

5. Persons found not guilty of a crime by reason of insanity (about 5 percent).
6. Persons convicted of a crime who were found to be mentally ill at the time of sentencing (about 5 percent).

Lanzkron (1964) described 150 patients admitted to Matteawan State Hospital in New York for a five-year period. They were charged or indicted for murder and represented about 5 percent of all murder cases occurring in New York State. Of the 150 cases, 79 percent or 118 were men, 32 were women, 86 were white, 41 Black, 18 Puerto Ricans, and 5 others. Before the commission of their crimes, 74 were married, 49 were single, 2 were widowed, 25 were divorced or separated, 92 were Catholics, 53 were Protestant, 4 were Jewish, and 1 was Greek Orthodox. Two-thirds of the group were between 21 and 45 years of age, 65 percent of the murders were committed by a gun or a knife, and 12 percent by strangulation. Thirty-two murdered their wives. Of the 32 women, six murdered their husbands. The patients also murdered their children, relatives, or friends. Thirty-nine of the 150 cases, however, murdered strangers. In other words, victims generally were family members. Previous hospitalization before committing the murder occurred in 42 percent of the cases and previous criminal records occurred in 46 percent. In 34 percent of the cases, intemperate use of alcohol was a contributing factor. Sixty percent of the cases exhibited average intelligence and the others were borderline or below. Fifty-three percent of the cases were unskilled workers. Twenty-five percent were diagnosed schizophrenic, paranoid type, and 23 percent were diagnosed psychoses with psychopathic personality. In 40 percent of the cases, homicide was a direct result of delusions of paranoia, and 60 percent of the cases committed homicide during a period of insanity or from motives and conditions that might influence sane minds, such as anger, jealousy, revenge, or robbery.

Concern has been expressed in the United States regarding criminal drug addicts. A study of criminal drug addicts (Messinger, 1965) indicated that of 6,039 examinations of criminal drug addicts, not one case of overt psychosis was found. Previous studies by other authors on different and smaller groups confirm this impression. During the six-year period of study, Messinger found only two cases of clinical psychoneurosis. However, 45 percent of the cases exhibited major character and behavior disorders. These were generally sociopathic, antisocial type (26 percent), inadequate and emotionally unstable personality (16 percent), and 40 percent indicated lesser character and behavior disorders, predominantly inadequate or aggressive in nature. In an earlier report, Messinger, summarizing statistical data on 57,000 persons involved in felonies, found only 4 percent significantly abnormal, either psychiatrically or psychologically.

On the other hand, an old study of sex offenders at Sing Sing Prison (MacCurdy and Lyons, 1950) indicated that everyone suffered from some type of mental or emotional disorder, although usually not so pronounced as to constitute mental illness. Almost all of the 102 men had histories of unfavorable childhoods with severe emotional deprivations. Irrationality of motivation and an overwhelming amount of hostility, often expressed in extreme brutality, were found. Most of the offenders displayed a hatred and resentment toward authority and persons representing authority. Alcoholism was associated in over half of the cases. The majority of the offenders possessed average intelligence.

There have been wide variations in clinical diagnoses of mentally disordered offenders. Kloek (1964) reported on 500 cases observed by him in 1964 at the Psychiatric Observation Clinic of the Dutch Penal System. The diagnoses of schizophrenia were considered in 30 cases, but only in one case was he absolutely sure of this diagnosis. Wiersma (1966) reported a similar finding. He quoted an article by Podolsky (1963) who stated that of the 3,000,000 college students in the United States, nearly 25 percent were schizophrenic. From this strong assertion, one might conclude that schizophrenics are rarely found among criminals in comparison to college students or to other "mental patients." McGee (1960) reported that of the 21,000 inmates in the California prisons, plus another 9,000 on parole, not more than 500 or 600 were diagnosed as psychotic. McGee further stated that only one out of 2,000 sex offenders against children examined during a three-year period at Bellevue Hospital in New York City was psychotic.

One must be cautious of these findings, however, because they may be a function of the inadequacies of psychiatrists in diagnosing rather than supportive of low incidence of schizophrenia. Clinicians diagnose on the basis of a few symptoms and if the patient does not exhibit these features, then he is not diagnosed as schizophrenic. Clinicians also may not recognize some of the schizophrenic cases because they may not develop until some years later. Antisocial behavior, however, is easily recognized by the community through observation of behavior which is defined as not acceptable. It matters less in which pigeon hole we place people than what it is we do for them. It is much more important to understand the etiology of their behavior than to classify them. The label schizophrenic may give us a false sense of security about our knowledge of mentally disordered offenders. The relationship between crime and personality changes associated with epilepsy have been thought important. Epilepsy has been associated with murder, arson, etc. Hill and Pond (1952) claimed some relationship between murder and epilepsy in the 105 cases of homicide that they investigated.

Lennon (1943) in an earlier article reviewed 5,000 cases of epilepsy and he found that few had acted in a violent manner and that none had committed murder. Allstrom (1950) found not one single murderer in fairly representative material of 897 epileptics. Within this group, acts of aggression constituted only 19 percent of the relatively small number of crimes committed by epileptics.

Some severe forms of psychiatric disorder may follow brain injury. Actual dementia is relatively rare, even after severe head injury. A study of 415 men (Hillbom, 1960) who had received a head injury in the Russian-Finnish War found that only 2 percent of the men suffered from dementia. The common complication was character change found in about 22 percent of the cases. There was a shift toward emotional lability, lack of foresight, and explosive behavior we associate with psychopathy. Little systematic work has been done on the complication of head injuries suffered in traffic accidents. The growing accumulation of brain injured traffic accident cases perhaps, with corresponding character changes, presents unexplored personal and social consequences.

The ages of mentally disordered offenders are interesting. Sexual offenders against young children occur later in life and are mainly first offenders. Some people believe that these offenses are the result of cerebral degeneration. A marked decline in the rate of criminal offenses with age runs parallel with a steep increase in the appearance of suicide and mental disorders. Rollin (1965) believed that crime is rare in old age. In one of his studies, there was a large discrepancy between the ages of patients officially admitted as mentally abnormal offenders and those admitted by ordinary civil procedures, who, as far as anyone knew, had not committed offenses. In the 30 to 50 year old age group, there were twice as many offenders as nonoffenders in contrast to the group over 60 years of age.

There are also variations in the incidence of schizophrenia as diagnosed in offenders in different countries. Cases in the United Kingdom indicate a range of schizophrenia between 60 and 90 percent. However, schizophrenia cases in Holland were only about 3 percent. A study by Dennissenko (1962) indicated that schizophrenia ranked first among mental patients whose acts constituted a danger to society manifested in threats of murder, attempted murder, and violent acts against persons. Cerebral arteriosclerosis ranked second.

At a psychiatric clinic in Sofia, Bulgaria, Schipkowensky (1956) found only 11 patients with cerebral arteriosclerosis out of 1200 patients admitted for examination. But he found 55 percent of his cases diagnosed as schizophrenic. In the Soviet Union, the diagnosis of schizophrenia ranged from 50 to 57 percent. At the New York Matteawan State Hospital, the diagnosis was made in 42 percent of the cases. Statistical data collected (de Reuck and Porter, 1968) at 73 psychiatric clinics and mental hospitals in Europe indicated schizophrenic diagnosis in 60 percent of the cases.

Gibbens (1959) confirmed many of the previous observations that psychopaths commit more aggressive offenses although the offenses may often be trivial. Aggressive crimes committed by neurotics, although fewer in number, are often more serious in nature. He claimed that recidivism among neurotics was quite low, representing only about 30 percent, as contrasted to psychopaths (about 60 percent). First convictions of psychopaths occurred later in life, at about 18 to 23 years of age, compared to neurotics who started as juvenile delinquents at about 12 to 16 years of age and had longer criminal careers. One thing that surprised Gibbens was how grossly disturbed a person could be without acquiring a criminal record. Gibbens suggests that criminologists probably overestimate the connection between psychopathy and crime.

Silverman (1946) studied 500 male psychotics consecutively admitted to the Medical Center for Federal Prisoners, Springfield, Missouri, from 1937 to 1941. His study indicates less insanity among Black prisoners than among whites. There were, however, some diagnostic differences between the races. Blacks were more commonly diagnosed as paranoid. Over half of the psychotics came from a rural or semi-rural background. Poverty, broken homes, parental abnormality, and lower educational achievement were more common in the backgrounds of the psychotics than in the normal federal prisoners.

Analysis of single maximum security institution by Dunham (1939) showed that 40 percent of the 543 male inmates committed for the first time between 1922 and 1934 to Illinois Security Hospital, Chester, Illinois, were diagnosed as schizophrenic, 13 percent were psychotic, 6 percent were paranoid, and 3 percent were psychopathic personality. In contrast, in 1971, 70 percent of the patients were diagnosed as schizophrenic, 11 percent as paranoid, and none were diagnosed as psychopathic. The crimes of inmates in 1927, in rank order, were murder, theft, burglary, and armed robbery. In 1971, it was murder, robbery, sex offenses, and assault, indicating more emphasis on crimes against persons. Today, the typical mentally disordered offender at Illinois Security Hospital comes from Cook County (Chicago), is unmarried, a non-veteran, Protestant, with a ninth grade education, about 30 years old, and he remains there for approximately eight months.

A study of 100 prisoners (Claghorn and Beto, 1967) in the Mental Treatment Center, Texas Department of Corrections, Huntsville, sheds some light upon people who mutilate themselves in a prison mental hospital. Subjects for the study were male convicts who were diagnosed as schizophrenic. The mean age of the men in the sample of 50 mutilators was 34 years. The first symptoms of mental illness occurred at about 25½ years of age. The average length of treatment in mental hospitals prior to arrest was eight months and the average time served in prison was about nine years. Very few Black prisoners were in the sample. Latin American men, however, made up a disproportionately large part of the group of mutilators. The authors argued that for the Latin male, prison is a more stressful situation than it is for other North American prisoners. The mutilators came from larger families than a matched cohort of nonmutilators. They also had a high rate of narcotic addiction if they were Latin American men. Sexual inadequacies or homosexuality were more common among mutilators, as was poor job adjustment.

Ninety-nine violent inmates were compared with 200 general psychiatric patients (Butler, Trice, and Calhoun, 1968). Thirty-three percent of the violent group were tattooed, compared with 12 percent of the general psychiatric patients. The content of the tattoos was very interesting. Twenty-three of the 32 male patients had a heart tattooed somewhere on their body distinguished with the words Mom, Dad, Mother, or some other form of parental reference.

One hundred five men, with one or more tattooes on their bodies, were compared with a control sample of untattooed men (McKerracher and Watson, 1969). The tattooed men were younger, more intelligent, and more aggressively unstable than the other patients. More cases of breaking and entering, larceny, drunken disorderliness, and attempted suicide occurred in their records.

A study (McKnight, 1963) of male offenders transferred from the correctional institutions to a mental hospital in Ontario, Canada, indicated that 75 percent of the patients were under 35 years of age, 33 percent came from broken homes, only 14 percent were married, 50 percent had less than an eighth grade education, 65 percent showed poor work records, and 19 percent indicated a history of alcoholism. Seventy percent of the patients also had prior experience in reformatories or penitentiaries. Half of the group from the penitentiary had previously shown symptoms of mental illness and had been treated for that in a mental hospital before incarceration in the penitentiary. Depressive, paranoid symptoms, and attempts or threats of suicide were the most frequent reasons for transfer to the mental hospital. Forty-five percent were finally diagnosed as schizophrenic, 20 percent were diagnosed psychopathic, and 6 percent were diagnosed as mentally deficient. The Canadian study found that male mentally disturbed offenders were approximately 31 years old, came from broken homes, were single, divorced, or separated, had an eighth grade education or less, held a number of jobs of short duration, probably had used alcohol to excess, and there was a strong likelihood that they had shown paranoid symptoms and/or depressive symptoms. At the Ontario Penitentiary, they probably had received drug therapy before being transferred to the mental hospital and their stay at the Ontario Mental Hospital was likely to average approximately seven months.

Satten (1965) believed that 5 to 10 percent of the 500 to 600 examined at a Reception and Diagnostic Center in Kansas were grossly mentally ill, yet the issue of sanity was never raised at their trials. He believed that many of these psychotic individuals could have been handled in regular correctional settings if the officials of those institutions had recognized that they were dealing with people who were sick instead of shipping such patients to and from special state hospital units. Treatment instituted in the prisons was in many cases sufficient to maintain these patients even when such treatment violated the traditional prison pattern of avoiding tranquilizers and medication. He thought that a trend was developing which encouraged prison people to take care of the so-called criminally insane. He said that they are not much different from normal criminals and that the people who are experts in the care of criminals are, perhaps, more expert in the care of the criminally insane. With the increasing voluntary nature of state hospitalization for other mental patients, our prisons will become treatment centers for mentally disordered offenders.

Hamburger (1967) suggested that penitentiary inmates have above average feelings of persecution bordering on the paranoia. He concluded that there was a more frequent pattern of paranoid symptoms in a penitentiary than in other clinical settings. The symptoms of the persecution syndrome found among inmates were as follows: a belief in the denial of due process of law; the defense lawyer in collusion with the district attorney; a prejudiced judge or jury; and unfair treatment by the warden, parole officer, or other staff members. Psychosomatic illnesses were common in many cases and directly related to fears of harassment by other inmates and officials (which might have some basis in reality).

The staff of the penitentiary was also influenced by the hostile and paranoid character of their charges. Custodial officers became very suspicious and developed a sense of danger working with prisoners. The officers' attitude contributed to a cycle of hostility, suspicion, fear, paranoia, more hostility, etc.

The outcome of mentally ill offenders is summarized in a study of two Maryland psychiatric populations in 1947 and 1957 (Rappeport, 1965). Comparison of their arrest rates with that of the general population indicated that for some serious offenses, the offender population had a higher arrest rate than the general population. There were no differences, however, between pre- and post-hospitalization arrest rates. A number of other studies have also shown very low arrest rates for discharged patients.

Rappeport's analysis (1962) of 73 patients showed that religious affiliation, sex, occupation, number of previous hospitalizations, age, history of excessive use of alcohol, diagnosis, educational level, or marital status were not significantly related to satisfactory post-institutional adjustment. However, the length of the last hospitalization was related. That is, if a person was in a mental hospital for less than one year, then he was more likely to make a satisfactory post-institutional adjustment.

Although the criminal justice system and mental health system run parallel with each other, they rarely integrate. The ways in which psychiatrists and lawyers attack problems are different because they have different value systems. Many of the differences have been resolved, but many more need attention. There are special problems in the gap between lawyers defending civil rights, and treatment-oriented, intuitive psychiatrists.

The difficulty in making sharp distinctions between normal, neurotic, psychopathic, and mentally disordered offenders should be reemphasized. The conditions most practitioners accept as illness, that is, serious brain damage or schizophrenia, really narrows the range within which individuals are free to make choices. Choice is obviously not completely free even in normal individuals. Moreover, the neurotic and the psychopath are simply variations from a norm. Hence, a line between different kinds of offenders cannot be very sharp.

In treating the seriously disordered offender, the schizophrenic, the manic-depressive, or the brain damaged, the straightforward aim may be to restore the individual as far as possible to a presickness state. In the case of a neurotic or a psychopath, however, the aims cannot be so easily stated. The relief of neurotic symptoms is not enough. In one way or another, the psychiatrist seeks to help this offender come to better terms with the society in which he lives. However, Wooton (1956) points out that psychiatrists do not question whether it is worth adjusting to society.

Analytic psychotherapy has not been very helpful for the mentally disordered offender. Most therapists work with the concrete aims of enabling the offender to get along better with others in his immediate environment. If a psychiatrist brings the offender to a position where the offender feels responsible for others and can experience guilt, the psychiatrist has obviously made a value judgment regarding the right of each individual to make moral judgments for himself. This may not be improper, but the fact that it is done must be explicitly stated. We must be clear about the character of our goals. The goals of treatment have to be specified because they raise difficult clinical, scientific, and ethical problems.

It is as Fink (1966) said, "The criminal mental patient is the neglected off-spring of psychiatry, labeled as psychotic, felonious, dangerous, anti-social, or violent." Relegated to penal institutions or to maximum security state institutions, the neglect of the essentially unique features of these patients, coupled with the usual restraint and isolation, perpetuates dependency, deterioration, and despair. The currently evolving philosophies liberalizing mental hospital procedures and practices is an attempt to emulate those aspects of the community that strengthen ego boundaries, that is, family contact, meaningful work, recreation, self-determination, etc. The mentally disordered offender has been generally excluded as not amenable or too dangerous, regardless of the diagnostic entity in which he is placed. His acting out in a violent and dangerous manner is the call for help that outrages society and demands retaliatory measures. His continuously extended ego structure fragments under inner and outer stress and he has few resources upon which he can draw to ameliorate or alter his personality structure. This disorganized personality must not be excluded from full utilization of all services featuring multidimensional approaches in a therapeutic community aimed at his rehabilitation.

REFERENCES

Abrahamsen, D.: *Crime and the Human Mind.* New York, Columbia, 1944.

Allstrom, C. H.: *Acta Psychiatr Neurol Scand, 35:*1, 1950.

Bluestone, H.: *Am J Correction,* 27:10, 1965.

Brodsky, Stanley: *Correctional Q, 1:* (in press).

Bromberg, W. and Thompson, C. B.: The relation of psychosis, mental defects and personality types to crime. *J Crim Law Criminol, 28:* 1937.

Butler, Joel R., Trice, John, and Calhoun, Karen: Diagnostic significance of the tattoo in psychotic homicide. *Correc Psychiatr J Soc Ther, 14:* 1968.

Casper, Elizabeth: Crime and mental illness. *Correc Psychiatr J Soc Ther, 11:* 1965.

Claghorn, James L. and Beto, Don: Self mutilation and a prison mental hospital. *Correc Psychiatr J Soc Ther, 13:* 1967.

Cook, Richard A.: Psychiatric Assessment of Military Offender. A paper presented at the Third Annual Conference of U.S. Army Clinical Psychologists. Chicago, 1960.

Denissenko, S. G.: In Questions of the Organization of Psychoneurological Assistance and Mental Prophylaxis. A symposium in Stravropol, U.S.S.R., 1962.

de Reuck, A. V. S. and Porter, Ruth: *The Mentally Abnormal Offender.* Boston, Little Brown, 1968.

Dunham, H. W.: The schizophrene and criminal behavior. *Am Soc Rev,* 1939.

Federal Bureau of Prisons: *National Prisoner Statistics: Prisoners in State and Federal Institutions for Adult Offenders, 1967.* 1969.

Fink, Ludwig: The criminal mental patient: the step-child of psychiatry. *Excerpta Medica,* Amsterdam, International Congress Serial #117, 1966.

Gibbens, T. C. N.: *J Ment Sci,* 104:108, 1959.

Hamburger, Ernest: Penitentiary and paranoia. *Correc Psychiatr J Soc Ther, 13:* 1967.

Hill, D., and Pond, D. A.: *J Ment Sci,* 98:23, 1952.

Kloek, J.: *Folia Psychiatr Neurol Neurocher Neerl,* 67:176, 1964.

Lanzkron, J.: *Correc Psychiatr J Soc Ther, 10:* 1964.

Lennon, W. G.: *Am J Psychiatr,* 99:732, 1943.

Lobenthal, J.: *Power and Put-on: The Law in America.* New York, Outerbridge & Dienstfrey, 1970.

MacCurdy, Frederick and Lyons, John A.: *Report on Study of 102 Sex Offenders at Sing Sing Prison.* New York, Albany, 1950.

Messinger, E.: A statistical study of criminal drug addicts. *Crime and Delinquency, 11:* 1965.

McGee, Richard: *Proceedings of the Symposium of the Mentally Abnormal Offender.* California, Department of Mental Hygiene, 1960.

McKerracher, D. W. and Watson, K. A.: Tattoo marks and behavior disorder. *Br J Crim, 9:* 1969.

McKnight, C. K.: Male patients transferred from reform and penal settings in Ontario to a mental hospital. *Can J Corrections, 5:* 1963.

Podolsky, E.: A note on the schizophrenic college students. *Am J Psychiatr, 119:* 1963.

Rappeport, Jonas R.: *Am J Psychiatr, 121:*776, 1965. *Am J Psychiatr, 118:*1078, 1962.

Rollin, Henry R.: The law and the mentally abnormal offender. *Ment Health, 24:*196, 1965.

Sadoff, Robert L.: *Correc Psychiatr J Soc Ther,* 17:1971.

Satten, Joseph: The criminal mental patient: a discussion. *Correc Psychiatr J Soc Ther,* 1965.

Scheff, Thomas: The role of the mentally ill and the dynamics of mental disorder: a research framework. *Sociometry, 26:* 1963.

Scheidemandel, Patricia L. and Kanno, C. K.: *The Mentally Ill Offender.* Baltimore, Garamond/Pridemark, 1969.
Schipkowensky, N.: *Clinical Psychiatry,* Sofia Naukai Izkustvo, 1956.
Silverman, Daniel: The psychotic criminal. *J Clin Psychopath, 8:* 1946.
Szasz, T. S.: The myth of mental illness. *Am Psychologist, 15:* 1960.
Wiersma, D.: *Excerpta Criminologica, 6:* 1966.
Wooton, Barbara: Sickness or sin. *20th Cent Mag, 159:*433, 1956.

Chapter 2

JUSTICE IN THE THERAPEUTIC STATE

Thomas S. Szasz

The writings of Thomas Szasz have shaken many of the traditions associated with the mentally ill. He has challenged us to ask many questions about these traditions. To him, the answers are obvious.

Editors

L aw and medicine are among the oldest and most revered professions. This is because each articulates and promotes a basic human need and value: social cooperation, in the case of law; health, in that of medicine. Simply put, the law opposes some types of social processes; it calls them crimes and inflicts punishment on those who commit them. Likewise, medicine combats some types of bodily processes; it calls them diseases and offers treatment to those who suffer from them.

To exist as a man, as a person, is synonymous with existing as a social being. The regulation of social relations is an indispensable feature of every society and, indeed, of every coming together of two or more persons. The concept of justice is thus necessary both for the regulation of human relations and for judging the moral quality of the resulting situation. This is what is meant by the statement that without law there can be no justice, but that the law itself may be unjust.

What constitutes justice varies from place to place and from time to time. This does not prove that the concept is devoid of meaning or is unscientific, as some contemporary social scientists claim. Instead, it shows that to the question, "What is a good or proper social order?" mankind has given and continues to give not one but many answers. For example, in principle, at least, capitalists believe that those who work harder, or produce more, or whose services are more valuable to the community should receive more for their work than those whose efforts are less productive. Communists believe that the products of all individuals should be pooled and distributed on the basis of absolute equality, and Marxists believe that labor and its products should be regulated by the formula "from each according to his abilities, to each according to his needs."

Framed as general rules of the game of life, contrasting concepts of justice, such as those listed above, would seem to have nothing in common. This is a fallacy. For underlying all concepts of justice is a notion so basic to social intercourse that without it life would promptly degenerate into a Hobbesian war of all against all. The notion common to all diverse concepts of justice is *contract*, the expectation that we shall keep our promises to others and they shall keep theirs to us. "It is confessedly unjust," wrote John Stuart Mill (1863), "to *break faith* with any one: to violate an engagement, either express or implied, or disappoint expectations raised by our own conduct . . ."

Why is contract so all important to human life? Because it is the foremost rational, nonviolent instrument for the equalization of social power. Contract is the social device par excellence that liberates the relatively powerless individual or group from domination by his more powerful superiors, thus freeing him to plan for the future. Conversely, lack of contract or systematic contract violation is an essential characteristic of oppression; deprived of the power to plan for the future, the inferior individual or group becomes subjected to the status derogation of dependency by his superiors. Thus, when the future arrives, the oppressed individual will be unable to care for himself and will be dependent on his protectors, for example, parents, politicians, psychiatrists.

To be sure, like all social arrangements, contract favors some members of the group and frustrates others. It favors the weak, that is, those who lack the power to coerce or, if they possess such power, the will to use it, and it frustrates the strong, that is, those who have such power or, if they lack it, strive to possess it. Generally, contract favors the child as against the parent, the employee as against the employer, and the individual as against the State. In each of these relationships, and in other similar situations, the superior member of the pair does not require contract to plan for *his* future; he can control his partner, by brute force if necessary. Contract expands the self-determination of the weak by constricting the powers of the strong to coerce him; at the same time, by placing the value of abiding by the terms of a contract above that of naked power and by universalizing this value, contract tames not only the power of the strong to coerce, but also that of the weak to counter-coerce.

In political life, the paradigm of contract is the Rule of Law, the principle that limits interference by the State in the conduct of the individual to circumstances that are clearly defined and known in advance to the individual. By avoiding lawbreaking, the citizen can thus feel secure from unexpected interference by State power. This arrangement may be contrasted with despotic or tyrannical government, whose principal characteristic in its dealings with the individual is not harshness but rather arbitrariness. The brutality and terror of this kind of political arrangement lies precisely in the utter unpredictability with which the police power of the State may be deployed against the individual.

One more example of the fundamental role of contract in the concept of justice should suffice. It is an ancient legal maxim (*nulla poena sine lege*) that there should be no punishment without law. The principle that a man should not be punished for an act which was not prohibited by law at the time when he engaged in it, shows dramatically that the concept of justice is rooted in ideas and sentiments that have more to do with the need to make behavior predictable than with the need to protect society from harm, for clearly a person may harm his neighbor without his behavior qualifying as an act prohibited by law. Today, a large part of what we call mental illness falls into this category of personal conduct. Arguing from the functional or scientific point of view, the modern psychiatrist or behavioral scientist would hold that what is or ought to be important here is the proper restraint and remotivation of the malefactor, not the abstract idea of justice. From his point of view, the pre-existence of law would not be a requirement for invoking the social sanction he calls psychiatric treatment. It is precisely at this point that the behavioral scientist applies the analogy between misbehavior and illness by arguing that just as a man may fall ill without his condition being officially recognized by medical science as a diagnosis, so, too, a man may in criminal conduct without his behavior being officially recognized by the law as a criminal act. In this view, what determines the existence of the undesired condition, whether it be illness or crime, and what justifies social intervention against it, whether it be treatment or punishment, is *the judgment of the expert, not a rule written down by lawmakers and legitimized by the judicial and political processes of government.*

These two fundamental principles of regulating human relations, the contractual and the discretionary, serve different aims. Each acquires its value from its function: to foster the individual's capacity for independence by enabling him to plan for the future in the case of contract; to enable the expert to act with optimal effectiveness by freeing him from the limitations of restricting rules, in the case of discretion. Since these are two radically different ends, it is hardly surprising that each requires different means for its attainment.

The impetus that drives men to depoliticize and therapeutize human relations and social conflicts appears to be the same as that which drives them to comprehend and control the physical world. The history of this process, that is, the birth of modern science in the seventeenth century and its rise to ideological hegemony in the twentieth, has been adequately set forth by others (Hayek, 1955, and Matson, 1964). I shall confine myself here to illustrating the incipient and developed forms of this ideology through quotations from the works of two of its most illustrious American protagonists, Benjamin Rush and Karl Menninger.

Benjamin Rush (1746-1813) signed the Declaration of Independence, was Physician General of the Continental Army, and served as Professor of Physic and Dean of Medical School at the University of Pennsylvania. He is the undisputed Father of American Psychiatry, and his portrait adorns the official seal of the American Psychiatric Association. Without comment, listed below are selected passages from Rush's writings showing how he transformed moral questions into medical problems and political judgments into therapeutic decisions.

> Perhaps hereafter it may be as much the business of a physician as it is now of a divine to reclaim mankind from vice (Rush, 1774).

> Mankind considered as creatures made for immortality are worthy of all our cares. Let us view them as patients in a hospital. The more they resist our efforts to serve them, the more they have need of our services (Rush, 1783).

> The excess of the passion for liberty, inflamed by the successful issue of the war (of Independence), produced, in many people, opinions and conduct, which could not be removed by reason nor restrained by government. . . . The intensive influence which these opinions had upon the understandings, passions, and morals of many of the citizens of the United States, constituted a form of insanity . . . (Boorstin, 1948).

> In the year 1915, a drunkard, I hope, will be as infamous in society as a liar or thief, and the use of spirits as uncommon in families as a drink made of a solution of arsenic or a decoction of hemlock (Binger, 1966).

> . . . Miss H.L. . . . was confined in our hospital in the year 1800. For several weeks she discovered every mark of a sound mind, except one. She hated her father. On a certain day, she acknowledged, with pleasure, a return of her filial attachment and affection for him; soon after she was discharged cured (Rush, 1812).

> Chagrin, shame, fear, terror, anger, unfit for legal acts, are transient madness. . . . Suicide is madness (Rush, 1810).

> Lying is a corporeal disease. . . . Persons thus diseased cannot speak the truth upon any subject (Rush, 1812).

> Terror acts powerfully upon the body, through the medium of the mind, and should be employed in the cure of madness (Rush, 1812).

> There was a time when these things [i.e. criticism of Rush's opinions and actions] irritated and distressed me, but I now hear and see them with the same indifference and pity that I hear the ravings and witness the antic gestures of my deranged patients in our hospital. We often hear of "prisoners at large." The majority of mankind are *madmen at large*. . . . Were we to live our lives over again and engage in the same benevolent enterprise [i.e. political reform], our means should be not reasoning but bleeding, purging, low diet, and the tranquilizing chair (Rush, 1951).

Rush's foregoing views provide an early nineteenth century example of the medical-therapeutic perspective on political and social conduct. His statements cited above amply support my contention that although ostensibly he was a founder of American Constitutional Government, actually he was an architect of the Therapeutic State (Szasz, 1963). The leaders of the American Enlightenment never tired of emphasizing the necessity for restraining the powers of the rulers, that is, for checks and balances in the structure of government. Rush, on the other hand, consistently advocated rule by benevolent despotism, that is, political absolutism, justified as medical necessity.

In summary, the Constitution articulates the principles of the Legal State in which both ruler and ruled are governed by the Rule of Law, whereas, Rush's writings articulate the principles of the Therapeutic State in which the citizen-patient's conduct is governed by the clinical judgment of the medical despot.

To bring into focus the ideology and rhetoric on which our present-day Therapeutic Society rests, I shall next present, in capsule form, the pertinent opinions of one of its foremost contemporary spokesmen, Karl Menninger, (1893-   ), a founder of the famed Menninger Clinic and Foundation, a former president of the American Psychoanalytic Association, the recipient of numerous psychiatric honors, and the author of several influential books in the mental health field. Like Rush, Menninger is one of the prominent psychiatrists in America. His views illustrate the contemporary psychiatric mode of viewing all manner of human problems as mental illnesses. Indeed, all of life as a disease requiring psychiatric care.

> . . . The declaration continues about travesties upon *justice* that result from the introduction of psychiatric methods into courts. But what science or scientist is interested in *justice?* Is pneumonia just? Or cancer? . . . the scientist is seeking the amelioration of an unhappy situation. This can be secured only if the scientific laws controlling the situation can be discovered and complied with and not by talking of justice . . . (Menninger, 1930).
>
> Prostitution and homosexuality rank high in the kingdom of evils. . . . From the standpoint of the psychiatrist, both homosexuality and prostitution—and add to this the use of prostitutes—

constitute evidence of immature sexuality and either arrested psychological development or regression. Whatever it may be called by the public, there is no question in the minds of psychiatrists regarding the abnormality of such behavior (Menninger, 1963).

In the unconscious mind, it [masturbation] always represents an aggression against someone (Menninger, 1964).

The very word *justice* irritates scientists. No surgeon expects to be asked if an operation for cancer is just or not . . . behavioral scientists regard it as equally absurd to invoke the question of justice in deciding what to do with a woman who cannot resist her propensity to shoplift, or with a man who cannot repress an impulse to assault somebody. This sort of behavior has to be controlled; it has to be discouraged; it has to be *stopped*. This (to the scientist) is a matter of public safety and amicable coexistence, not of justice (Menninger, 1938).

Eliminating one offender who happens to get caught *weakens* public security by creating a false sense of diminished danger through a definite remedial measure. Actually, it does not remedy anything, and it bypasses completely the real and unsolved problem of how to *identify, detect, and detain potentially dangerous citizens.*

(In a society properly informed by "behavioral science"), indeterminate sentences will be taken for granted, and preoccupation with punishment as the penalty of the law would have yielded to a concern for the best measures to insure public safety, with rehabilitation of the offender if possible, and as economically as possible.

Being against punishment is not a sentimental conviction. It is a logical conclusion drawn from scientific experience. It is also a professional principle; we doctors try to relieve pain, not cause it.

The principle of *no* punishment cannot allow of any exception; it must apply in every case, even the worst case, the most horrible case, the most dreadful case—not merely in the accidental, sympathy-arousing case.

All of the participants in this effort to bring about a favorable change in the patient . . . are imbued with what we may call a *therapeutic attitude.* This is one in direct antithesis to attitudes of avoidance, ridicule, scorn, or punitiveness. Hostile feelings toward the subject, however, justified by his unpleasant and even destructive behavior, are not in the curriculum of therapy or in the therapist. . . . Doctors and nurses have no time or thought for inflicting unnecessary pain even upon patients who may be difficult, disagreeable, provocative or even dangerous. It is their duty to care for them, to try to make them well, and to prevent them from doing themselves or others harm. This requires love, not hate.

Do I believe there is effective treatment for offenders . . . ? *Most certainly and definitely I do.* Not all cases, to be sure. . . . Some provision has to be made for incurables—pending new knowledge—and these will include some offenders. But I believe the majority of them would prove to be curable. The willfulness and the viciousness of offenders are part of the thing for which they have to be treated. They must not thwart our therapeutic attitude. It is simply not true that most of them are "fully aware" of what they are doing, nor is it true that they want no help from anyone, although some of them say so.

Some mental patients must be detained for a time even against their wishes, and the same is true for offenders (Menninger, 1968).

As the foregoing quotations show, Menninger focuses systematically on the offender or alleged offender, who, in his view, is either punished with hostile intention or treated with therapeutic intention. Accordingly, he urges that we abandon the legal and penological system with its limited and prescribed penalties and substitute for it a medical and therapeutic system with unlimited and discretionary sanctions defined as treatments.

For centuries, the enlightened and scientific behavioral technologist has thus sought, and continues to seek, the destruction of law and justice and their replacement by science and therapy.

Those who see the main domestic business of the State as the maintenance of internal peace through a system of just laws justly administered and those who see it as the provision of behavioral reform scientifically administered by a scientific elite have two radically different visions of society and of man. Since each of these groups strives after a different goal, it is not surprising that each condemns the other's methods. Constitutional government, the Rule of Law, and due process are indeed inefficient means for inspiring the personality change of criminals, especially if their crime is not shoplifting, which is Menninger's favorite example, but violating laws regulating contraception, abortion, drug abuse, or homosexuality. Similarly, unlimited psychiatric discretion over the identification and diagnosis of alleged offenders, coercive therapeutic interventions, and lifelong incarceration in an insane asylum are neither effective nor ethical means for protecting individual liberties of insuring restraints on the powers of the government, especially when the individual's illness is despair over his inconsequential life and a wish to put an end to it.

In conclusion, the legal and the medical approaches to social control represent two radically different ideologies, each with its own justificatory rhetoric and restraining actions. It behooves us to understand clearly the differences between them.

In the legal concept of the State, justice is both an end and a means. When such a State is just, it may be said to have fulfilled its domestic function. It then has no further claims on its citizens, save for defense against external aggression. What people do, whether they are virtuous or sinful, healthy or sick, rich or poor, educated or stupid, is none of the State's business. This, then, is a concept of the State as an institution of limited scope and powers. In such a State, the people are, of course, not restrained from fulfilling their needs, not met by the State, through voluntary association.

In the scientific-technological concept of the State, therapy is only a means, not an end. The goal of the Therapeutic State is universal health, or at least unfailing relief from suffering. This untroubled state of man and society is a quintessential feature of the medical-therapeutic perspective on politics. Conflict among individuals, and especially between the individual and the State, is invariably seen as a symptom of illness or psychopathology, and the primary function of the State is accordingly the removal of such conflict through appropriate therapy, therapy imposed by force, if necessary. It is not difficult to recognize in this imagery of the Therapeutic State the old inquisitorial, or the more recent totalitarian, concept of the State, now clothed in the garb of psychiatric treatment (Szasz, 1970 a,b).

REFERENCES

Binger, C.: *Revolutionary Doctor: Benjamin Rush, 1746-1813.* New York, Norton, 1966.

Boorstin, D. J.: *The Lost World of Thomas Jefferson.* Boston, Beacon, 1948.

Hayek, F. A.: *The Counter-Revolution of Science: Studies on the Abuse of Reason.* New York, Free Press, 1955.

Matson, F.: *The Broken Image: Man, Science, and Society.* New York, Braziller, 1964.

Menninger, K.: *Man Against Himself.* New York, Harcourt, 1938.

———*The Crime of Punishment.* New York, Viking, 1968.

———*The Human Mind.* New York, Literary Guild, 1930.

———*The Vital Balance: The Life Process in Mental Health and Illness.* New York, Viking, 1963.

———*The Wolfenden Report: Report of the Committee on Homosexual Offenses and Prostitution.* New York, Stein, 1964.

Mill, J. S.: *Utilitarianism* (1863). In Lerner, M. (Ed.): *Essential Works of John Stuart Mill.* New York, Bantam, 1961.

Rush, B.: Lecture on the medical jurisprudence of the mind (1810). In Corner, G. W. (Ed.): *The Autobiography of Benjamin Rush: His "Travels Through Life" Together With His "Commonplace Book for 1789-1812.* Princeton, Princeton University Press, 1948.

———*Letters of Benjamin Rush, Volume II.* Princeton, Princeton University Press, 1951.

———*Medical Inquiries and Observations upon the Diseases of the Mind (1812).* New York, Hafner, 1962.

———Letter to Granville Sharp, July 9, 1774. *American Studies, 1:*20, 1967.

———Letter to Granville Sharp, November 28, 1783. *American Studies, 1:*20, 1967.

Szasz, T. S.: *Ideology and Insanity.* Garden City, Doubleday-Anchor, 1970a.

———*Law, Liberty, and Psychiatry: An Inquiry into the Social Uses of Mental Health Practices.* New York, Macmillan, 1963.

———*The Manufacture of Madness.* New York, Harper, 1970b.

---

*Part of this paper was published in the *Indiana Law Review.*

Chapter 3

THE LAW ENFORCEMENT OFFICER AND THE MENTALLY DISORDERED OFFENDER

SENECA H. NOLAN, JR.

Seneca Nolan views the problems of the mentally disordered offender from a rather unique perspective. As an attorney for the Metropolitan Police Department, City of St. Louis, he is concerned with the impact this special population has on the police officer's role and his ability to carry out his duties. He makes some specific suggestions for the criminal justice system in order that the needs of the mentally disordered offender and the law enforcement officer can be met in a complimentary fashion. Some of the problems for both groups which can be created or solved by legislation are also discussed.

EDITORS

I will not attempt to explain the degrees of mental disorders. Nor will I present a survey of current criminal laws which relate to mentally disordered offenders. Rather, I will try to present the factual effects such theories and laws have on daily police work.

Before developing this theme further, it seems appropriate to outline the general state of the law applicable to mentally disordered offenders.

In the United States, four basic tests have been developed to determine criminal responsibility. They are the M'Naghten Right and Wrong Test, the Irresistible Impulse Test (used in conjunction with the M'Naghten Test), the Durham or Product Test, and the American Law Institute's Model Penal Code.

The oldest (1843), and by far the most generally used, test in this country is the M'Naghten Rule. In this case the English House of Lords stated the following:

> . . . to establish a defense on the ground of insanity, it must be clearly proved that, at the time of the committing of the act, the party accused was laboring under such defect or reason, from dis-

ease of the mind, as not to know the nature and quality of the act he was doing; or, if he did know it, that he did not know he was doing what was wrong.

The M'Naghten Rule has been subjected to repeated criticism as being outmoded and unrealistic. The Rule was based on nineteenth century concepts of mental capacity which have been universally rejected today. Furthermore, it requires medical matters to be discussed in terms of "right and wrong." The psychiatrist is forced to give testimony in terms that have very little meaning to him and have no meaning in the clinical study of the defendant's mental condition.

Because of the medical argument that an individual who can distinguish between right and wrong might still be unable to refrain from doing a forbidden act, a number of states have added the Irresistible Impulse Test to the M'Naghten Rule. The exact language varies from state to state, but the general holding is that, although there may have been a capacity to distinguish right and wrong as to the particular act, the defendant still is not responsible if by reason of mental disease he was irresistibly impelled to do the act, though he may have known that the act was wrong.

The third test, known as the Durham Rule, is the least accepted by the courts, but the favorite of defense attorneys. The Durham Test requires that two elements exist: a mental disease or defect and a critical relationship between the disease and the act. If the criminal act was the *product* of the mental disorder, then no criminal responsibility exists. The Durham Rule is premised upon the theory that there is no adequate legal test for insanity and, therefore, it is best handled as a question of fact for the jury to determine. This test is often criticized as being so vague as to be useless. The mere fact that certain acts were committed is often enough to cause some juries to conclude that anyone who would do such things has to be mentally ill.

The final test used in this country, and the one adopted in essence by Missouri, Illinois, and other states, is the one contained in the Model Penal Code. For example, the Missouri law provides the following:

> A person is not responsible for criminal conduct if at the time of such conduct as a result of mental disease or defect he did not know or appreciate the nature, quality or wrongfulness of his conduct or was incapable of conforming his conduct to the requirements of law.
>
> The terms mental disease or defect . . . do not include an abnormality manifested only by repeated criminal or otherwise antisocial conduct . . .

As it can be seen, Missouri has codified the M'Naghten Rule and included the central theme of the Irresistible Impulse Test. Missouri's test is considered a well-worded compromise between the extreme strictness of M'Naghten and the vague, undefined latitude of Durham.

Another major change in Missouri's law brought about by the Model Penal Code was the establishment of standards for determining whether the defendant possessed the necessary state of mind required by the law as an element of the particular criminal offense.

The theory underlying this test of responsibility is often referred to as the Doctrine of Diminished Responsibility. Missouri's statute reads as follows:

> Evidence that the defendant did or did not suffer from a mental disease or defect shall be admissible.
>
> (1) To prove that the defendant did or did not have a state of mind which is an element of the offense; or
>
> (2) For the purpose of determining whether or not the defendant if found guilty of a capital offense, shall be sentenced to death or life imprisonment.

A number of states have enacted statutes designed to cope with sex offenders who, because of a psychopathic condition, commit or have a tendency to commit sexual crimes. The statutes generally recognize that the sexual psychopath is neither mentally normal nor legally insane and for that reason requires special consideration, both for his own sake and for the protection of society. Such statutes are not criminal statutes. They provide civil commitment, segregation, and treatment of the sexual psychopath rather than criminal punishment. These statutes were enacted for the purpose of preventing persons suffering from mental disorders, though not insane or feebleminded, from being punished for crimes they commit during the period of such ailments. The social objective of such statutes is twofold: to protect society by sequestering the sexual psychopath so long as he remains a menace to others and to subject him to treatment to the end that he may recover from his psychopathic condition and be rehabilitated.

In 1949, Missouri enacted its Criminal Sexual Psychopaths Law. Under this law, when any person is charged with a criminal offense and the prosecuting official has reason to believe the person is a sexual psychopath, he shall file a petition to that effect with the court. Missouri requires a pending criminal charge, while other states permit a petition being filed without a criminal charge as a condition precedent. Once the petition is filed, a copy is given to the person charged and a hearing is set. If at the hearing *prima facie* evidence of his propensities is presented, the court must appoint two qualified physicians to examine the person charged. Upon completion of their examination, the doctors are required to file with the court a report of their examination and findings. If the report of one of the two examining physicians establishes the fact of a mental disorder, the court shall order a second hearing. At the second hearing, the court at its own discretion or at the request of the person charged, may order a jury for the determination of the issues.

Illinois enacted a similar law in 1965. It differs from Missouri in two major areas. Illinois requires the appointment of two psychiatrists and makes the use of a jury mandatory. Under both states' procedures, the individual charged is represented by counsel and may offer evidence in his behalf. Because these hearings are considered civil rather than criminal, constitutional safeguards against self-incrimination and evidence of other crimes do not apply. This permits the State of Illinois to offer not only the information provided by the person charged to the examining doctors, but also evidence of prior acts or convictions. In Missouri, if the person is found to be a criminal sexual psychopath, the court may commit him to the state hospital until such time as "his release will not be incompatible with society." However, any release will be conditioned upon a minimum probation of three years. Further, while the person is hospitalized, an annual medical report must be filed with the court.

The constitutionality of the State, through its police powers, legislating special treatment for the sexually dangerous person, has been upheld. The United States Supreme Court held that the sexual psychopath or the sexually dangerous person does constitute a dangerous element which the State, at its discretion, could put under appropriate control.

Although the rationale underlying both Missouri and Illinois law is constitutionally acceptable, numerous commentators have objected to its practical applications. The major objection is the commitment of the individual beyond the maximum sentence permissible if he had been convicted in a criminal trial. Secondly, the possible use of the sexual psychopath law where insufficient evidence exists to gain a conviction in a criminal trial.

Missouri also provides authority to permit police officers to have an individual temporarily confined in a hospital when the officer believes the individual may harm himself or others. This statute provides as follows:

> Any health or police officer may take an individual into custody, apply to a hospital for his admission and transport him thereto for temporary confinement if such officer has reason to believe that
>
> (1) The individual is mentally ill, or is a mentally retarded person at least seventeen years of age and not under the jurisdiction of a juvenile court, and, because of his mental condition, is likely to injure himself or others if allowed to be at liberty pending examination and certification by a licensed physician . . .

This procedure can be compared with that of Illinois. There, a court order is needed to take an individual into custody under an emergency admission procedure and transport him to a hospital for admission. To obtain such a court order, a petition, together with a physician's certificate, must be filed with the court. If satisfied that the welfare of the patient or the general public requires it, the court may then order the person admitted to a hospital.

Such a procedure does not meet with a great deal of support from police officers, and it is understandable why more practical means are found. Thus, a criminal or quasi-criminal charge is often used to gain "lawful custody" of an individual for the purpose of achieving his confinement.

In light of the aforementioned, we can see that no unified legal procedures exist in this country for coping with, or providing for, the mentally disordered offender. Further, in my experience, it would appear that no consensus exists in mental health circles as to the preferred course of treatment (both legal and medical) of the mentally disordered offender.

It is not surprising then to find that police officers are not as knowledgeable or as progressive in this area as many of us would have them. But before criticizing them, we should be prepared to walk in their shoes.

The average City of St. Louis police officer is 36 years old. He has been with the department for 11 years, and he is paid $9,800 a year. One hundred and fifteen of the officers have completed 60 hours of college credits or more, while 196 have not completed high school; the remainder are high school graduates.

The police officer in today's society does not have the luxury of time to reflect on his work. When called upon, his duties demand that he respond and react quickly. Without the benefit of sufficient formal training, we cannot expect him to respond or act as a mental health therapist.

Further, all of the laws outlined earlier, with the exception of Missouri's Temporary Custody Law, have application only *after* responsibility for the individual offender has passed from the police to the prosecutor. The police officer is thus compelled to treat the majority of offenders as criminal suspects, regardless of their mental state. Exceptions to the usual arrest procedures occur only when the individual's behavior is so unusual or bizarre as to compel the police officer to conclude that he is mentally ill.

The effect of the present state of law and medicine is such that it permits only two classifications by police officers: mentally disturbed individuals and criminal suspects. Thus, police officers tend to treat all offenders as criminals, including the mentally ill.

I would now like to express my thoughts on what is required to aid police officers in dealing effectively and humanely with the mentally disordered offender. These suggestions are presented in the order of assistance most readily available under existing circumstances. They may not correspond to each locale's priority of needs.

Adequate training must be provided for the police officer to permit him to recognize and handle *all* mentally ill persons. Such a program can be met through films, books, and manuals. As useful as these tools are, they should not take the place of actual classroom training. Live exchanges greatly improve the rapport between police officers and mental health specialists, and they should be made available whenever possible.

Such training, however, is useless unless each community has adequate provisions for professional services to respond to psychiatric emergencies. This commitment requires money and the services of trained personnel. Facilities must be opened and staffed to provide psychiatric assistance 24 hours a day, seven days a week. Additionally, every state should enact a law similar to Missouri's Temporary Custody Law to permit police officers to have an individual confined in a suitable medical environment for psychiatric evaluation.

The final suggestion I would make is the most difficult to implement and, perhaps, is not even factually justified. I would urge that a program of study and evaluation be undertaken to determine whether the sociopath should be removed from the criminal justice system.

In my judgement, no other mentally disordered personality presents such a serious threat to our society. As the number of such offenders increases before our courts, we witness an increase in the volume, seriousness, and senselessness of their crimes. Victims of robberies are shot so that additional time may be gained for escape. In the City of St. Louis, recently, a 17-year-old girl had her eyes slashed out so that she would be unable to identify her assailant in a robbery—a man she knew by name. It is no wonder that police officers felt frustrated and provoked when they learned that the 30-year-old suspect had been convicted of first degree robbery in 1959, followed by a second armed robbery conviction from which he was on parole at the time of this robbery.

The laws of Missouri and Illinois, indeed those of most states, have provisions to exclude sexual psychopaths from prisons and to commit them to hospitals for treatment. But no state has broadened its laws to permit the treatment and confinement of the sociopathic personality that does not commit sexual crimes.

Hervey Cleckley (1964), in a book titled *The Mask of Sanity*, summarized the characteristics of the psychopathic personality as follows:

On-the-surface charm, and seems rather bright.

No symptoms one would find in a person who is mentally ill.

No nervousness of the sort commonly seen in a neurotic patient.

Unreliable—you can't depend on him. He will make promises, but not keep them.

Untruthful and insincere.

Lack of any feeling of shame after he has done something wrong.

Anti-social behavior which often doesn't make sense.

Poor judgment and failure to learn from experience.

Think only in terms of how things affect him personally; cannot really love another person.

Lack of any real feelings for the rights of others.

Lack of realization that there is something wrong with him. It is always somebody else's fault.

Callousness and lack of ability to work harmoniously or in a team with others.

Foolish behavior with drink or even without it.

Threats of suicide when in trouble—seldom carried out.

Sex life—superficial, and often promiscuous.

Failure to follow a life plan.

With such character traits, it is easy to see why sociopathic personalities constitute a threat to themselves and to others. The solution to this problem is not one of simply insuring law and order, but rather protecting the welfare of both society and the individual.

Before concluding, I would like to quote from a study undertaken by the American Psychiatric Association (1966) regarding police efficiency in responding to mental health emergencies. These few words state quite eloquently the true function of the police officer as he relates to the mentally disordered.

> Among the various people we interviewed, we encountered a variety of attitudes toward the police, although for the most part comments were favorable. At their best, policemen appear to respond well, when confronted with persons they can clearly identify as sick and in need of help. Of the two prevailing images of policemen, namely, the punitive and the helping, many of them appear to prefer the helping role. And, even when they are not trained very much, if at all in this aspect of their work, they function very well. They are often especially effective with mentally ill people from the lower socio-economic groups, for while these groups are ambivalent toward policemen, they tend to turn to them when in distress. A study in one city of medium size found that more than half of the telephone calls received at the complaint desk of the police department did not concern crime but were pleas for help from people who were in some kind of trouble.

REFERENCES

American Psychiatric Association: *Psychiatric Emergency.* Washington, D.C., 1966.
Cleckley, Hervey: *The Mask of Sanity,* 4th ed. St. Louis, Mosby, 1962.

Chapter 4

DETERMINATION OF COMPETENCY— BURIAL AT THE CROSSROAD

ROBERT E. SCHULMAN

Doctor Robert Schulman is both a practicing clinician and an attorney. As such, he is uniquely qualified to address himself to the issues, both clinical and legal, present in the determination of competency to stand trial. A major premise in the paper is that competency to stand trial interferes with the goal of criminal law. Specifically, Doctor Schulman charges that we have, "regardless of how unwillingly it has come about, a collusive collaboration exists between law and medicine (including the behavioral sciences) which effectively buries the patient alive." He characterized the behavioral scientist as the grave digger and the attorney as the pallbearer. Some timely suggestions for change are presented.

EDITORS

We all bring different experiences and biases to the issue of competency to stand trial. In an effort to insure that we all have some of the same basic information concerning this issue, I will begin with some definitions, propose a few legal and psychological issues, and endeavor to place the problem in a psycholegal framework.

The great number of people affected by the question of competency to stand trial is often not realized. A determination of incompetency is one of the most frequent reasons for hospitalization of persons involved in the criminal justice system. A large study of offenders (Scheidemandel and Kanno, 1969) admitted to more than 50 facilities across the country revealed that questions regarding competency were the reason for hospitalizing 52 percent of the offender-patient population. Among the same group, only 4 percent of the patients were individuals found not guilty by reason of insanity. On the basis of the sample in this study, it is speculated that across the nation at any given time, there are about 15,000 persons hospitalized who are waiting return for trial or discharge.

In terms of sheer numbers of individuals affected by questions of competency to stand trial, the problem is of substantial magnitude. Aside from the question of how many people are affected, the underlying psychological and legal issues present interesting and important questions. As a matter of fact, when one considers this issue, one needs to examine the underpinnings of the criminal law process and the relationship of this process to the behavioral sciences. Competency to stand trial is one of three points in the criminal justice system where behavioral science input has had an important, if confusing, impact. The issue of competency to stand trial is just as important as are questions regarding culpability or mental condition at the time of execution of sentence. Nevertheless, competency has received less attention and is less well understood by lawyers and behavioral science experts who serve the court.

Before considering these three intrusions into the legal system by behavioral science experts, a further preliminary statement must be made. The most difficult and confusing aspects of the issue of competency to stand trial are highlighted by trying to come to grips with the idea that mental illness per se is not the same as, or equal to, incompetency to stand trial. A finding that a person is mentally ill, even severely ill, does not answer the question of whether that person is capable of standing trial. On the other hand, the person who is not mentally ill may not be capable of standing trial either. The clearest case of a person incompetent to stand trial is the one where the patient is immobilized and totally unable to communicate with his attorney. He is, therefore, clearly unable to assist counsel in providing information necessary for the preparation of his case. Among the mentally ill group, the catatonic individual, for example, would fit this category. On the other hand, certain paranoid individuals with delimited and circumscribed delusional systems might be quite able to assist counsel in preparing a defense. Certainly, the patient's assistance to the attorney would be hampered if the paranoid delusional system intruded on reality to such an extent as to make the patient unreliable. Absence of mental illness does not necessarily mean that a person can or will assist in his defense.

The person who willfully, stubbornly, and unwaiveringly refuses to communicate with his attorney may be incompetent to stand trial. Yet, that individual, while possibly being eccentric, might not be pigeonholed into any of our traditional psychiatric diagnostic categories. A finding of mental illness all too often has been equated with incompetency to stand trial. The primary reason for this confusion lies in the law which does not concretely spell out standards to be used in determining competency to stand trial and has left the criteria vague (Robey, 1965). Where the law has been definite, the behavioral science expert has distorted the criteria to fit an illness model.

The issue of competency to stand trial developed out of our English Common Law tradition which required that an accused person have the capability to adequately defend himself against his accusers in a court of law. Common law criteria for determining this was whether or not the defendant understood the nature of the legal process, recognized the consequences that could follow from the accusations made against him, and had the ability to assist his legal counsel in his own behalf.

FOLIE À TROIS

Insanity at the Time of Trial

Under contemporary law, and not much different from the common law tradition noted above, a person is eligible for trial if he is able to understand his position and to participate rationally and adequately in his defense. In part, this rule is formulated out of humane considerations and an extension of the prohibition against trials *in absentia*. The reason is that the mentally incompetent defendant, although physically present, is actually mentally absent and unable to help in his defense. The Illinois Code (Illinois Revised Statutes, Chapter 38) which is based on the American Law Institute's Model Penal Code is illustrative of the usual statutory provisions for competency:

A. If before a trial or after a judgment has been entered but before pronouncement of sentence, or after a death sentence has been imposed but before execution of that sentence, the court has reason to believe that the defendant is incompetent, the court shall suspend the proceedings and shall impanel a jury to determine the defendant's competency. If a jury is waived by the defendant, the court shall conduct a hearing to determine the defendant's competency.

B. If, during the trial, the court has reason to believe that the defendant is incompetent, the court shall suspend the proceedings and shall conduct a hearing to determine the defendant's competency and shall, at the election of the defendant, impanel a jury to determine that issue.

C. The burden of going forward with evidence of the defendant's incompetency shall be on the party, if any, requesting that determination.

D. The court may appoint qualified experts who shall be compensated by the county to examine the defendant with regard to his competency and to testify at the hearing. Any party may introduce, at the hearing, other evidence regarding the defendant's competency. No statement made by the accused in the course of any examination into his competency provided for by this Section, whether the examination shall be with or without the consent of the accused, shall be admitted in evidence against the accused on the issue of guilt in any criminal proceeding.

E. If the defendant is found to be competent, the proceedings which had been suspended shall be resumed.

If the defendant is found to be incompetent, he shall be committed or remain subject to the further order of the court in accordance with Section 104-3 of this Code.

The determination called for by the above procedural rule is guided by the following which, while purporting to define competency, sets out the general common law understanding of competency:

For the purpose of this Article, "incompetent" means a person charged with an offense who is unable because of a mental condition:

a. To understand the nature and purpose of the proceedings against him; or

b. To assist in his defense; or

c. After a death sentence has been imposed, to understand the
nature and purpose of such sentence.

If before a trial, or after a judgment has been entered but before
pronouncement of sentence, or after a death sentence has been
imposed but before execution of that sentence, the court has reason
to believe that the defendant is incompetent the court shall suspend
the proceedings and shall impanel a jury to determine the defendant's competency.

The judicial interpretation of the test for competency to stand
trial has presented inconsistencies. For example, in a case where
an individual had, because of brain injuries, blunted affect and
dulled emotional awareness, a Massachusetts court (Commonwealth v. Harrison, 1961) held that even if the defendant was
emotionally blunted, if he was aware and understood cognitively
his position relative to the accusations against him and was
cognitively able to assist in his defense, then in spite of the absence of emotional elements, the individual would be deemed
competent to stand trial. On the other hand, some cases (U. S. v.
Chisholm, 1904 and Dusley v. U. S., 1960) hold that affective as
well as cognitive appreciation is required for the individual to
be deemed competent to stand trial.

The behavioral scientist's usefulness to the court may be
facilitated by thorough understanding of the rule and implemen-
tation of the criteria Robey (1965) has suggested be used to
gauge an individual's competency to stand trial. Under the general heading of comprehension of court proceedings, the behavioral scientist should consider the individual's awareness of
his surroundings, procedure, principals, charges, possible verdicts,
penalties, and legal rights. The individual should have the ability
to advise counsel regarding facts, plea, and, in a limited way,
legal strategy. The defendant should be able to maintain a relationship with the lawyer, maintain a consistent defense, should
know when and which rights he is waiving, be able to interpret
witnesses' testimony, and be able to testify if that were necessary.
Another aspect which is important, but often overlooked, is the
individual's susceptibility to decompensation while awaiting or

standing trial. With regard to possible decompensation, Robey suggests that violent individuals, those suffering acute psychosis, suicidal depression, regressive withdrawal, or organic deterioration may be the ones most susceptible to decompensation prior to trial.

The behavioral scientist's *raison d'être* in this framework can only be to furnish information to the court on these issues. Even this more limited involvement is questionable, but may be justified under special circumstances. The behavioral scientist should furnish facts upon which the court, with other information, may base its conclusion. If the behavioral scientist views his task in this light, Robey's guidelines may be helpful.

At this point, I want to briefly note the two other junctures in the criminal justice system where behavioral science input frequently is found. This, I believe, is important to do for clarity and to help us keep in mind the important distinction between these three legal tests.

Insanity at the Time of the Offense

Simply put, the behavioral scientist, and again most often the psychiatrist, is asked to testify whether or not the accused knew that what he was doing was wrong. It is at this juncture and not the juncture where competency to stand trial is determined that the well-known tests of criminal responsibility are applied. There has been a great deal of quibbling and rhetoric over the M'Naghten Rule and the so-called refinements found in the Durham adaptation of the M'Naghten Rule. We are aware that well-informed and articulate behavioral scientists have criticized and taken serious issue with behavioral science input at this point in criminal proceedings (Szasz, 1963; Menninger, 1970).

The American Law Institute's Model Penal Code has proposed the following rule:

    1. A person is not responsible for criminal conduct if at the time of such conduct as a result of mental disease or defect he lacks substantial capacity either to appreciate the criminality of his

conduct or to conform his conduct to the requirements of the law.

2. The terms "mental disease" or "defect" do not include an abnormality manifested only by repeated criminal or otherwise antisocial conduct.

Insanity at the Time of Execution

The law provides that an insane man cannot be executed, while a sane man can. The test is that the condemned person must realize that he is going to be punished for a crime he has committed. The behavioral scientist again is in a peculiar position in that if the man is not competent to be executed, then the task is to rehabilitate the individual so that he can be executed. This, of course, leads to a certain kind of nauseating absurdity and, to the best of this writer's knowledge, the issue of insanity at the time of execution is not raised frequently.

GAMESMANSHIP

Anyone, anytime, and in any manner may raise doubt concerning the individual's competency to stand trial. The degree of evidence required to proceed is minimal, and if any doubt at all is presented by either the defense or the prosecution, the court must then make some determination of the defendant's competency to stand trial. As a practical matter, ordinarily this issue is raised by the defense counsel and any simple statement to that effect is sufficient to raise the doubt. Once the issue is raised, whatever proceedings have been initiated are staid and a competency examination completed. Ordinarily, the cost of a competency examination is paid by the state.

Typically, defense counsel proceeds with a written motion asking for a competency examination. Following this motion, the court issues an order specifying that a particular physician or physicians who are disinterested and qualified experts determine the defendant's mental condition at the present time and report to the court regarding the individual's competency. The reports provided by the examining physician or physicians are frequently terse, unimaginative, and bland documents that would not pass critical scrutiny if it were not for the judge's acceptance and willingness to tolerate conclusions and lack of factual statements in the reports. Courts frequently do not pay close attention to the nature and extent of the examination that is completed. In most instances, the court asks the examiner to answer the ultimate question of responsibility. A well-documented psychiatric report may be criticized by the court if it does not directly answer the legal test. There is no clearer abdication of responsibility by the court than in this instance. All too often, the examiner believes that he is functioning under the M'Naghten Rule and confuses the determination of competency with the responsibility question. In addition, the examiner frequently does not clearly understand that mental illness in and of itself is not the criteria for the determination of competency to stand trial. If both of these confusions exist in the mind of the examiner, then he is more likely than not to find the individual incompetent; not because this is actually the case, but because the examiner's confusion leads him to err on the conservative side. The maxim is "when in doubt, hospitalize for longer period of examination." The examiner believes that there is little to lose in doing this and ordinarily does not envision himself as abridging the individual's constitutional rights. Indeed, frequently the defendant may wish to postpone the trial and determination of guilt or innocence.

The criminal law, as all law, is designed to dispose of cases and controversies. The question of competency to stand trial interferes with that goal. Competency examinations may be nothing more than a device for both sides to find out something more about the individual's personality. Supposedly, this additional information helps both sides in considering plea bargaining and reaching some disposition prior to trial. In this sense, a competency proceeding is a discovery procedure used by both sides to buttress respective plea bargaining positions. The defense attorney may resist competency examinations particularly where he believes that his client has an excellent insanity defense. In this situation, the defense attorney does not wish to have the client to stand trial at the present time even if his condition is less than adequate. Proceeding to trial when the defendant is not competent and the attorney is aware of the defendant's incompetency is tantamount to perpetrating a fraud on the court. If the client is incompetent but the attorney proceeds to trial, this violates the principle that a court does not want to proceed against an individual who is not mentally present. On the other hand, when the defense attorney anticipates the insanity defense case may be weak or not sufficiently persuasive, he may want a competency hearing as a way of buying time. During the delay, the prosecution, judge, and community may change their attitudes about the crime or defendant. Competency hearings, unfortunately, can move in the direction of becoming hearings to determine responsibility. In this summary procedure, the case is frequently heard before the judge without a jury and inappropriately goes beyond the limits to which it should be confined. Too often, the court decides too early that the defendant is not responsible. Convincing the court that the defendant is incompetent strengthens an otherwise weak insanity defense. This opening gambit is a device to have the court begin thinking about the defendant as a flesh and blood human being rather than just a felon. This is a softening-up tactic. When this defense maneuver is successful, the prosecution then is willing to have the client committed and often willing not to prosecute the case at all.

If the prosecuting attorney anticipates an insanity defense, he may raise the question of competency to stand trial to begin demonstrating that the psychiatric arguments about mental illness are without substance or merit. The prosecutor often knows that the individual will not submit to an examination conducted by prosecution psychiatrists when an insanity defense has been raised. Thus, the examination to determine competency to stand trial may give the prosecutor some information that he would not otherwise have.

The tactical and strategic movements by the attorneys on both sides can be justified or rationalized from a variety of different perspectives. It is critical, however, to recognize that the reasons for asking for any psychiatric examination often have nothing to do with the mental health of the individual, but are part of the gamesmanship employed in the prosecution and defense of criminal cases.

When the individual is found competent to stand trial the prosecution is resumed. This may result in an insanity defense, negotiated plea contingent upon treatment, or a conviction and sentence. If the individual is found incompetent to stand trial, ordinarily he is committed to a maximum security hospital for treatment until such a time that he is restored to competency. Commitment for custodial purposes only without attempts to rehabilitate and restore the individual to a competent state would be punishment without trial and is unconstitutional. Unfortunately, long custodial commitments frequently are the result of competency proceedings, not because of any malicious intent on anyone's part, but because most maximum security hospitals, or similar type institutions, while purporting and desiring to provide treatment, have few qualified staff to implement treatment.

When the individual is restored to competency, in the opinion of the hospital staff and treating physicians who are supposed to make that decision, he is to be returned to the court. Too often, however, it is not clear to the treating physician that he has this responsibility. Even if it were clear, the physician may be unwilling and unprepared to take the responsibility for returning the individual to court. First, the physician may be uncertain about what restored to competency really means. Secondly, if he does understand what restored to competency means, he may be unclear as to which condition the individual is supposed to be restored. Finally, if he understands the first and second of these problems, he may be reluctant to return the individual to the court because he realizes that if the individual is found guilty of the alleged act and placed in a prison, this is not going to do much for the individual's mental health which is probably tenuous anyway. It is easy then, for the physician to avoid taking any action and to believe that it is better to keep the individual in the hospital where he is being treated than do something that might result in a conviction and incarceration in a penal institution.

McGarry (1965) recently has reported findings which indicate how decisions concerning offender-patients are reached by the staff of psychiatric institutions. McGarry concluded that generally psychiatrists appear to view psychotics as incompetent to stand trial and reach their decision within an exclusively medical framework. He further notes that due process of law may be compromised where the importance of the issue is not understood by the examiner. Thus, certain constitutional rights like a speedy and prompt public trial may be denied the individual. McGarry also concluded on the basis of his limited sample that the courts ordinarily accepted a psychiatrist's judgment with regard to the issue of competency to stand trial and thus aid and abet the psychiatrists' use of a medical model for determining what indeed is a legal issue.

Generally, a person may be returned to court in two distinct manners. He may receive from the rehabilitating institution a bill of health stating that he is restored and he is now competent to stand trial. This route out of the hospital is contingent upon overcoming the many constraints of releasing and finding offender-patients restored. Institutions vary in their procedure for doing this. It may be one physician's responsibility or it may be delegated to a committee. The other way a person may obtain his release is via the route of *habeas corpus* through the courts. In such a proceeding, the patient, as the petitioner, asks the court to issue a writ of *habeas corpus* directing the hospital to show why the inmate should be continued in custody. If the hospital is unable to do that, then the individual must be returned to the court for trial or be released. The *habeas corpus* route for the individual is not easy and a great deal of pressure is put on him not to pursue this remedy. If the individual is able to execute his writ of *habeas corpus*, it is likely to be heard before a judge who is already influenced and guided by the hospital staff. This in turn makes it easy for the hospital staff to justify continued hospitalization.

Giving all sides the benefit of sound and ethical intentions, we nevertheless, regardless of how unwittingly it has come about, have a collusive collaboration between law and medicine (including the behavioral sciences) which effectively buries the patient alive. The grave diggers are the behavioral scientists. Just why the behavioral scientist is involved in the competency issue is not any clearer than why he is involved elsewhere in the criminal law process. At other junctures in the criminal justice system, however, the psychological issues seem more definite, even if camouflaged and distorted by the M'Naghten Rule or other tests of insanity and responsibility. Here we have a simple question to be asked and answered. Any of us, without any special expertise, it would seem, would be able to answer the question. The lawyer himself is probably in the best position to answer and determine whether or not the particular individual is able to communicate the kind of information that is necessary to effectively aid and assist in his defense and understand the proceedings against him.

If the behavioral scientist is the grave digger, then the lawyer, through his relatively passive and placid role, is the pallbearer. The incantation is played through the righteousness and dignity that only courts can muster. Following the ritual, the incompetent individual is buried and lost in the labyrinth of hospital systems. Indeed, he is at the crossroad—not prisoner, not patient, but someone in between, unable to get help, someone without a definite status. The hospital staff experience him as an unnecessary burden, not a good patient, but a person who is there under duress, unwilling to cooperate and participate in treatment. Frequently, the hospital staff's attitude is such that it makes it impossible for even a cooperative offender-patient to benefit from the milieu treatment. The staff are put in a bind as well. If they do treat him, to what end? To rehabilitate him to stand trial and then possibly face imprisonment is not a task to which many treators aspire. The individual hospitalized as a result of a competency hearing is in quite a different position from the person acquitted by reason of insanity and then hospitalized. When the individual has been acquitted he no longer is an offender-patient. It is easier to view him as a patient with expectations that through treatment he can begin to lead a productive, responsible life. The person found incompetent to stand trial has the worst of all worlds. His fate has not been decided. He is detained and committed to a place which is supposed to provide help, but which views him with suspicion, distrust, and fear.

In the past, individuals who suicided were punished or were punished further by unholy interment—burial at a crossroad without distinctive marking. I do not mean to suggest that pleading incompetency to stand trial is suicidal, yet it does not get the individual very far. If not a dead end, such commitments most often turn out to be a long delay. This delay may actually deprive the individual of needed treatment as well as cause delays in the legal system.

Some study (Lipsitt, 1971) has been given to the application of objective measures to determine competency. These efforts are worthwhile but do not solve the problem. Behavioral scientists, as well as lawyers, need to be made aware of the actual consequences of a finding of incompetency and the little utilitarian value of such a proceeding. Application of behavioral science technology in the legal arena should be limited to the dispositional phase of the legal process and not at those points in the proceedings which deal with legal responsibility and purely legal issues. Since the question of competency is basically a jurisdictional question and not dispositional, the behavioral scientist's role could be eliminated. Responsibility for the competency proceeding needs to be returned to the appropriate keepers of that trust. This is a question the lawyer must answer. Only the lawyer knows whether or not his client is able to assist, cooperate, and understand the legal issues. Lawyers, in turn, must avoid using the competency issue as a maneuvering, dilatory device and, instead, face the problem squarely. The legal profession must no longer support and encourage attorneys in this avoidance. To do so makes a mockery of two systems, each of which in its own way is able to serve the offender-patient.

REFERENCES

Commonwealth v. Harrison. 173 N.E. 2d 87 342 Mass. 279. 1961.

Dusky v. U. S. 362 U. S. 402. 1960.

Lipsitt, P. D.: Competency for trial: a screening instrument. *Am J Psychiatr,* *128*:137, 1971.

McGarry, L. A.: Competency for trial and due process via the state hospital. *Am J Psychiatr, 122*:623, 1965.

Menninger, Karl A.: *The Crime of Punishment.* New York, Viking, 1968.

Robey, A.: Criteria for competency to stand trial: a checklist for psychiatrists. *Am J Psychiatr, 122*:616, 1965.

Scheidemandel, Patricia L. and Kanno, C. K.: *The Mentally Ill Offender.* Baltimore, Garamond/Pridemark, 1969.

Szasz, Thomas: *Law, Liberty, and Psychiatry: An Inquiry into the Social Uses of Mental Health Practices.* New York, Macmillan, 1963.

U. S. v. Chisholm. C. C. 149 F. 284. 1904.

Chapter 5

A LAWYER VIEWS MENTAL HEALTH PERSONNEL

JOSEPH S. LOBENTHAL, JR.

Joseph Lobenthal is an articulate and provocative attorney whose concern with our criminal justice system has been documented in his previous publication, (Power and Put-on: The Law in America, 1971). In his paper, he rather forthrightly discusses the role of the mental health professional and the attorney. He separates the processes and goals of these two groups and discusses them in light of the needs of the system, the client, and the professional. He avoids using the traditional, emotional, and inaccurate arguments that so often confound the real issues present in our adversary system. In conclusion, he presents his suggestions about the proper role of the psychiatrist in the courtroom and how he might behave in order to have his opinions become more meaningful to the legal process.

EDITORS

B efore discussing my view of the relationship obtaining between lawyers and mental health personnel, it seems necessary to briefly refer to one important difference between the *systems* of law and psychiatry whose interactions create this relationship. For the purposes of this paper, the term psychiatry will be used to include the several mental health disciplines.

Both criminal and civil law are, essentially, an action and dispositive process. That is, law is concerned with doing something then and there about the situations and people before it, with disposing in one way or another of some present conflict. It has to decide, for example, what to do with the deviant and disorderly person, and to do so in such a way that will satisfy, or at least be tolerated by, those persons who are the law's constituency. Only secondarily, and apart from the way decisions are actually made, does a supposedly logical framework exist in order to justify whatever action law has taken. On this plane alone is law concerned with verbal formulations.

51

Many people, however, mistake legal words, both statutory and decisional, for the deed. That is, they study these words literally instead of seeing them as a functional part of a dispositive ritual. It is for this reason that they become overly concerned with words. They do so in order to persuade themselves of the law's predictability and rationality; essential elements of legal effectiveness that are thought of as consistency; what practitioners call *stare decisis,* or the doctrine of following precedent. Attempts are made to fit facts to word formulations in order for both lawyers and lay persons to perceive what is going on as predictable and rational, and to think that what will happen in one case is based on, or is at least related to, what was decided in similar ones in the same jurisdiction or was prescribed in like cases previously resolved before a higher appellate court.

Lawyers and judges, as well as legal writers, in short, legal professionals and apologists, are occupationally concerned with explaining the law in terms of a rationale or some legal doctrine or theory. They cannot be blamed for doing so, however, for the bulk of the training they received was in the study and use of these verbal formulations. Moreover, in practice they acquire a vested interest in sustaining the mystique of law as a conceptual edifice.

The fact is, however, that verbal formulations in law accompany or immediately follow, but do not predetermine or underlie, the decisional or dispositive process. It is easier to understand this when we consider the illustration of lawyers' briefs. The only time there are two sides to any story is when there are two parties to a dispute. When there are more than two parties, there are more than two formulations. Each competes with the other and is submitted in support of a particular desired result. There are any number of theories available or potentially able to be formulated. One merely selects from or assembles them depending on his desired end. Not only are there all kinds of theories but, depending on how they are arranged in an argument, their uses are multiple—any fact situation can be made to yield practically any result. Furthermore, in the almost never-never case in which only one verbal formulation, or just a few possible alternative ones seem to be available, what any one of these is actually held to mean when applied to the facts of the litigation depends on a virtually unlimited universe of human interpretations and on the social and psychological complex in which these facts have arisen and are presented.

Stated more concretely, what is on everyone's mind—the judge's, the jury's, the lawyer's, the client's, and, in certain cases, the public's—is one thing only, outcome or disposition, and not the formulation by which this outcome is reached.

By contrast to the task and approach of law, the field of mental health, especially when they interact with the legal process, are by and large not immediately dispositional. They are, instead, predominantly concerned with formulation, with the conceptual and the verbal, with the diagnosis of a personality, with a statement of how past experiences brought an individual to his psychological present, and with a description of the symbolic significance for him of a particular act, or of the role of a certain individual in his life. This field can afford to have its action aspects determined by its verbal formulations or theories because of the time intervening between its action (for example, therapy) and its results (for example, improvement in a disordered personality). Consequently, the mental health field almost by definition must take its formulations seriously. Such formulations are, in fact, the greatest part of what practitioners have to rely on in order to inform others what they are doing, to make their activities professional.

From such formulations, the field of criminology has received several psychological constructs called typologies. These, perhaps, help explain, and to some extent they are also useful as predictive instruments. However, except those that are so obvious and almost simpleminded as to be truistic, I believe their reliability is questionable because outcome in the case of any individual is normally dependent on the occurrence or absence of external or social events rather than on variables which are specific to the mental health fields.

In any case, these formulations are the sort of contribution which law may reasonably expect from the field of mental health.

There is also limited legal use for them, given the fact of the different functions of verbal formulations in the two systems, as has just briefly been described. I believe, however, that a misunderstanding exists between practitioners in law and psychiatry. Each fails to appreciate that their counterparts will utilize formulations according to the needs of his own system. In other words, lawyers expect psychiatrists to comply with the law's request for guidance not as psychiatrists but as lawyers. They are always disappointed when they find psychiatrists acting instead like psychiatrists. The converse is also true. Psychiatrists never cease to wonder and to be disappointed when they discover that their lawyer colleagues have responded to psychiatric reports and testimony as lawyers instead of as fellow psychiatrists.

From the lawyer's viewpoint, these psychiatric formulations do not really help with the legal task of deciding what should be done with such fundamental issues as what is the right or just—or, if you will, suitable and appropriate—solution to a particular, immediate conflict. Mental health formulatons do not tell us, for example, whether or not an individual's liberty should be curtailed or revoked and, if so, for how long, in what sort of setting, under and dependent on what conditions, and, most importantly, they do not tell us why such-and-such social response is imperative, given the competing interests on hand.

In short, the various helping and human service professions that have arisen from the study of behavior are more descriptive than prescriptive. These professions are concerned with formulations and their actions are slow. Psychiatric formulations are supposedly a basis on which long-term personality and characterological changes may be effected.

The law, on the other hand, is primarily dispositive. Therefore, it must be authoritarian, moralistic, and punitive. Its formulations deal not with rationality but with rationalization, with hot and pressing issues such as the extent to which professed social norms should be reconciled with practice, with pragmatic decisions about balancing competing claims of searchers after power, and with what is necessary to keep a pluralistic society reasonably manageable nominally under the single roof and rule of federal, state, or local governments. Since law is immediate and action oriented, its verbal formulations, unlike those in the mental health field, far from being central, come only after the decisional facts.

As Thomas Szasz and others have pointed out, however, psychiatry and the mental health professions have a sort of handmaiden function in the law. This function is to lend the weight of their formulations as pseudo-authoritative reasons for the law's doing whatever it has a mind or finds necessary and expedient. It is here, so they say, that mental health best fits into the adversary judicial process.

It is not my intention to discourse on this well known thesis by Dr. Szasz. I should like, however, to point out that it is a thesis that most sophisticated practitioners, both in law and in mental health, have come to accept as describing how things actually are.

For example, one of our most eminent jurists, Judge David Bazelon of the United States Court of Appeals, a man whose decisions have contributed substantially to what many consider an enlightened forensic psychiatry, has stated that "The big terms of a psychiatrist's discourse under any rule (or formulation, of mental responsibility) are large, ominous-sounding words, words which no one else in the courtroom really understands and which, as time goes on, clever lawyers are becoming quite adept at proving that the psychiatrist himself did not fully understand."

Similarly, Dr. Karl Menninger has written that "Psychiatrists can say that a man is distracted or deluded or hallucinated, but whether or not the state of mind is compatible with legal competence is something about which psychiatrists have only common knowledge and not scientific."

My own book (Lobenthal, 1971) also seeks to illustrate some of these notions from the different and distinct viewpoint of a legal practitioner.

To dissipate any impression that this current of opinion runs only in one direction, there are, to be sure, still a number of reputable mental health persons who take the position that penal judgments should be almost exclusively a matter of psychiatric determination and discretion. Renatus Hartogs, for example, the psychiatrist who predicted on the basis of a rather brief observation of the young Lee Harvey Oswald that the boy was then and would continue to develop as a dangerously assaultive human being, takes a different point of view. Dr. Hartogs is the Chief Psychiatrist of the Probation Department for the courts of New York City, a former senior psychiatrist at Sing Sing Prison, and the author of a book on psychiatry and crimes of violence. His view is that a person should be incarcerated or involuntarily hospitalized not necessarily on the basis of any antisocial acts already committed but, instead, on the basis of a psychiatric judgment that he is or upon the happening of certain social or psychic conditions and events, is reasonably likely to become dangerous to society.

Dr. Hartogs further believes that such an individual, whether or not he has committed a crime, should be kept in restraint for as long as some psychiatric opinion exists that his condition is unchanged or, put another way, while the individual remains either potentially or actually dangerous. Of course, Hartogs' viewpoint raises profound questions about one's legal rights and of the desirability of government having this power and control over individual freedom and liberty. It seems safe to say that what Hartogs advocates, Szasz fears we are now dangerously close to having. Besides these questions, however, Hartogs presupposes a degree of reliability in psychiatric judgments dealing with the future and a consensus about the meaning of the term dangerous which the rest of us would find acceptable.

In one sense, the question of dangerousness or the degree of social risk which is involved when one or another sort of crime or criminal is unpunished but treated is precisely the one question to which judges and juries, at least subliminally, if not officially, address themselves when they decide either to accept or reject a defendant's request to be treated as insane. Hartogs is willing to trade the present ration of social stability, such as it is, that we have because the general public now decides how much vengeance it needs to exact and under what conditions it will waive its right to determine the parameters of tolerable deviance. For this, he would exchange what he says is a higher degree of reliability in predictions about a person being a danger to society than we have at present by letting psychiatrists determine who should and who should not be punished, how, and for how long.

To the extent that Hartogs' psychiatrists would be making so-called scientific and medical judgments, these primitive and fundamental components of a penal system, vengeance and the appearance of controlling deviance, would become irrelevant. To the extent that psychiatrists simply reflect existing social norms and values in their decisions, they would be little different from a lay jury except that their very presence on the scene would serve as a kind of conscience balm permitting some to delude themselves into believing that a new and civilized jurisprudence was at hand.

Two views have been mentioned. One is that psychiatry has no place in either a civil or a criminal court. The other is that judges and lay juries have no competence or entitlement to arbitrate the conflicting testimony of psychiatric experts. There is also a middle ground to the effect that psychiatric determinations should be made only after a judgment of guilt has been rendered on the facts and should extend, through the means of indeterminate sentences, to what happens to a convicted person during the period of his restraint and to when that person is released from prison.

Whichever one of these positions one adopts does not, from a lawyer's point of view, amount to a hill of beans. The perspective of most legal practitioners is that it makes little difference whether one's jurisdiction has the M'Naghten, Durham, the American Law Institute rule or, as we have in the State of New York, a modified M'Naghten insanity criterion. Of course, these formulations are interesting to debate, but they are not really relevant to the lawyer in action. For him they are like other formulations used in law, to be applied in explaining the disposing result which he advocates. His technique is to elicit the correct or statutory wording from the expert on the witness stand. Whatever the statute might say, that is what he wants the jury to hear. This is done for only one purpose—to unlock appropriate feelings so that the required number of jurors will conclude that his client is or is not the sort who should go to jail or trial. In other words, the expert testimony at a minimum must recite what the statute requires and beyond this it must also reach the jurors as rhetoric on a nonintellectual level.

The legal system maintains its credibility by purporting to hold accountable only those who knowingly and wittingly did whatever it was that is proscribed, who possess what lawyers call *scienter,* that is, knowledge of some sort or another or a sense of awareness. This means that it is not overtly conceivable that we proceed against someone who was beyond an acceptable pale of rationality at the time the criminal act was committed. Nor can we proceed with a trial to determine the facts of a crime and, thereafter, resolve the issue of a defendant's mental capacity to have understood the trial proceedings. Before a trial is conducted, the law requires a finding, once the issue has been raised, that the defendant is able to comprehend the proceedings against him and to aid in his own legal defense. Until the issue is raised, the required mental condition is assumed to exist. It would be manifestly unfair and uneconomical to have trials and then to decide retrospectively that the first finding was invalid because the defense was not able to have the aid of the defendant himself.

The above is true all the way along the line. For example, a defendant may have been found sane at the time he committed the act, at the time of his trial, and then be sentenced to death. That sentence may not be carried out if he is found later to have become insane until a competent psychiatric authority rules that he has gained his sanity once again. I am not aware of any case in which a condemned man escaped execution by this device although I have read innumerable accounts of persons who seem, by my lay standards, to have suffered extreme and excruciating personality changes while in solitary confinement or en route to the execution chambers. So far as I can tell, the proceedings were not halted while a psychiatrist was called in to render an opinion about whether this behavior, under the circumstances, was normal or whether the person in question had become insane.

The point is, of course, simply that psychiatric opinions, verbal formulations in the law to the contrary notwithstanding, are to be understood as useful only in the social context of the particular proceeding that is going forward. Lawyers are only incidentally interested in the intrinsic content of psychiatric formulations. They are mainly concerned with these formulations to the extent that there is a use for them within the scope of the judicial process on hand and so that they can win.

What is necessary, therefore, in criminal cases, is expert testimony essentially parrotting or paralleling whatever statutory formulation of responsibility a particular jurisdiction has in effect. Everything else is gilding the lily and anything less, no matter how sincere, is useless.

When a lawyer goes shopping for a psychiatrist who will testify, for example, that his client was insane at the time of the act or, in a civil case, that the deceased had testamentary capacity and competency, what he wants to generate is a cloud of verbiage that will accomplish his client's wishes of freedom, in the one case, and probate of the will in the other. He does not care, nor is it his job to do so under an adversary system, what the so-called truth is, not because he is indifferent to it but only because, at that point, it is the jury's job to decide between conflicting versions that are being propounded by experts on the subject of this particular sort of truth. The lawyer's own personal morality is discussed later.

Nor, in my opinion, do most of these experts themselves believe in the formulations about which they testify. Mental health personnel who are contacted by a lawyer generally read the signals or, to mix metaphors, the code between the lines of cross-professional dialogue. They know perfectly well what they are being hired to say. If they do not say it, then they are quite naturally weeded out of the case before the time for their testimony is at hand. They are even impatient with members of their own profession when the lawyer representing their side has been so inept as to call another psychiatric witness whose lack of advocacy or partisanship jeopardizes his own client's case.

Under these conditions, the roles of lawyer and mental health expert soon merge. That is, most lawyers must become versed in the jargon of the mental health expert in the same way that a lawyer picks up some of the argot and knowledge of, say, an orthopedist or a neurologist after a few years of trial practice. Conversely, the more expensive mental health witnesses are not only facile in the idiom of their field but can also be counted on to be in command of certain legal skills that will protect their testimony. For example, they can anticipate what is coming and keep their cool under the fire of cross-examination.

A lawyer seeking to destroy, as the legal profession refers to this process, the credibility of an opposing expert has available to him the same sort of litigation aids that exist with respect to other fields of expert testimony. In a recent symposium, for example, one well-known psychiatrist deplored as outrageous the fact that in order to remain on top in the courtroom, he had found it necessary to invest in a treatise, written for the legal profession as a guide to cross-examination. He purchased this work in order to master and thereby learn how to avoid the slings and arrows and the traps and pitfalls of opposing lawyers' questioning.

My point is that every lawyer wants to win for his client. His own attitudes, to a limited extent, serve as a brake of sorts on his ability to proceed with just anything the client wants or to always look for the most lenient disposition of a case. This brake can be adjusted, however, by money or psychic income such as publicity or prestige. In order to win, it is in the nature of the lawyer's business to enlist the aid of whatever experts he requires and are available. He, himself, also becomes superficially knowledgeable in their field. Psychiatric testimony has taken on the coloration of every other sort of courtroom testimony. Perjury is not encouraged but, in the mental health field, neither is it absolutely necessary, because what is involved is a matter of opinion rather than some sort of psychic litmus test.

As we witness the escalation of courtroom pyrotechnics, with lawyers becoming skilled in psychiatry and psychiatrists versed in the law, several questions quite naturally arise. What, exactly, is being accomplished by all this folderol? Is the role of a mental health expert in the courtroom in expounding formulations of psychic conditions or disability simply that of pander to the highest bidder? What about these carefully worded formulations that take up so much time in interdisciplinary legislative committees and are so hotly debated in academic circles? How are issues of competency and sanity actually decided if the words bandied about are simply window dressing?

I think most of the answers to these and similar questions are to be found not just in an examination of the courtroom format, upon which we have concentrated so far in this presentation, but in the dynamics of our adversary system of resolving conflicts. From an attorney's point of view, if one side's psychiatric expert neutralizes the other's, then what is left is the "gut feeling" of members of that time tested highly questionable institution, the jury. Juries have to decide what they want done with the person in the dock, whether he should be punished or, as many of them see it, let off and eventually returned among them without punishment.

It is my experience that in those cases where the circumstances of a crime has been so heinous or bizarre as to indicate almost *prima facie* that the perpetrator must have been abnormal, defense lawyers are most reluctant to raise the sanity questions and juries are even more reluctant to go along with an insanity verdict. The reluctance of the lawyers can often be attributed to their own assessment of their chances of success. There seems to be a strong feeling in cases like those of Leopold and Loeb, Sirhan Sirhan, Jack Ruby, and Charles Manson, as well as others that are not equally complicated by sensationalism, that particularly violent or out of the way crimes will be punished, that psychiatric testimony, findings, or even pleas of insanity and lack of full responsibility should be rejected as inconsistent with a desired penal disposition.

There are, then, at least two reasons why many lawyers are reluctant to raise the responsibility issue where it seems, on first blush, most suitable. These are the lawyer's sense of what judges and juries will tolerate; and their subconscious sharing of attitudinal norms. There seems to be an unspoken fear that we might approach a time when, in order to get off, all a defendant need prove is that his crime was incomprehensible to the average lay juror. On the basis of similar reasoning, it has been held that evidence of repeated criminal acts, no matter what the psychological import and implications of the repetitive nature of these acts, cannot, by itself, be used to indicate such psychopathy or sociopathy as will exonerate a defendant from criminal responsibility.

By the same token, juries seem more receptive to psychiatric testimony when crimes of excessive viciousness and violence are not involved, where violence has been family or friend directed, or in other situations that do not seem to threaten either the norms and safety of jurors themselves or the sanctity of some of their more highly regarded social institutions. In fact, certain crimes of violence that are popularly believed to have been committed in defense of these institutions are almost synonymous with the easy-out of legal irresponsibility. The classic example which comes to mind is that of the husband who happens upon his wife and her lover in bed, who forthwith dispatches one or both of them, and who is then acquitted, almost automatically in some jurisdictions, on mental grounds. Since the felon in this case is supposed to have done what was eminently sensible and what every red-blooded American would do in defense of honor and the institution of home and hearth, it is hardly to be believed that any jury seriously regards him as having been insane when the crime was committed. This illustration points up the real feelings in American law that insanity is a label that should be reserved in certain cases for persons who are precisely not insane but for whom we need to find a way to avoid punishment. Thus it is that psychiatrists and jurors sometimes operate on vastly different wavelengths.

Lawyer selectivity with respect to utilizing the formulations and, therefore, the services of mental health personnel also works the other way. In the lower criminal courts of any large or medium-sized American city, one sees many hundreds, if not thousands, of defendants each day being processed through our criminal justice system. Many of these defendants may well be mentally and/or organically ill by most laymen's standards, most legal formulations, and any current medical definition. For the most part, these people are low resource individuals who are, for various reasons, casualties of modern and, in particular, urban living. Some of them can be seen practically fully evolved in urban elementary schools, youths who are hyperkinetic, talk to themselves, and seem filled with a stifling rage and distorted (but certainly not normative) perspective of those around them and of life and society in general. Getting back to their adult counterparts, many of those whom we see in court look stunned, diseased, dazed, and uncomprehending. They stare blankly, speak incoherently, if at all, and often in monosyllables, walk in a hunched and withdrawn manner, and display other manifestations of peculiarity that contrast with the mien and level of seeming awareness of lawyers representing and prosecuting them as well as of the jurists and jurors who will hear the charges against them and decide their fate. They seem to come from and live in a mental and emotional world different from that by whose processes and in accordance with whose standards and values their behavior is going to be judged. They are, finally, of little help to their lawyers in assisting in the preparation of their own defense and this, as much as the better known huge caseload of public defenders, accounts for the paucity of many such defenses.

From this group, therefore, one might expect a raft of insanity pleas and claims that defendants are incompetent to stand trial. Yet, such is not the case, and sanity and competency issues are seldom raised, although incompetency gets more defense attention than does the plea of insanity. Most often, instead, we see the bargaining process at work, pleas of guilty, either as charged or to a lesser included offense, in exchange for agreements by the prosecution not to oppose defense counsel's request for a suspended (supervisory) or minimum sentence.

There seem to be three factors involved here. First, for relatively minor charges many lawyers believe that their clients are better off in jail for a short time, or on the nominal kind of probation our lower courts require, than to undergo the experience of an observational period followed by a commitment for treatment which would likely be much longer than the probable maximum sentence for the offense itself. At the end of the line, too, these clients, after being declared cured, might have to face trial after all, or what is more common, the state would resist their release nominally on the grounds that a cure had not been effected, but actually because the prosecutor no longer had the evidence to bring the case to trial and felt disinclined merely to dismiss it.

Second, in addition to the human and emotional costs of a determination of incompetency or insanity when facilities for observation are provided free by the state, the results are usually negative. Success requires recourse to the private sector of mental health practitioners. The monetary cost of such a determination, when private psychiatric witnesses are obtained, is relatively high. Realistically, then, this route is normally available only in cases involving middle-class offenders who, coincidentally, constitute the class of patients that can most frequently be treated successfully and who then, after a reasonable time, find themselves released.

Lastly, lawyers recognize that an insanity plea for most individuals of the sort we are discussing would be an exercise in futility, even if legally successful. Permanent social management of these individuals seems unnecessary because periodic short sentences amount to almost the same thing and it is a fact that members of this population are among the regulars who provide lower criminal courts with their business.

It may be helpful to rephrase these three notions. The insanity or incompetence bulwark is like the tip of an iceberg for the defendant who prevails in his claim. The decision to take refuge behind this bulwark is a matter of tactics and strategy, not science. As such, it bears a relationship to whatever financial, personal, and social resources are available to the defendant rather than, or at least in addition to, his actual mental condition. For example, it is ironic but true that it is hard to prepare an insanity defense without the cooperation of the defendant himself. Thereafter, costs can be reckoned in terms of a financial burden on the state, of the deprivation of a person's liberty for an indeterminate time, and a perceived threat to society when certain individuals are not convicted despite their being put out of circulation.

Probably, we can count among the effects of this last-mentioned concern the decision of many lawyers not to make use of the incompetent-to-proceed-at-trial approach for defendants of the type we have been discussing. In many states, this is far more readily granted than a defense of insanity. Officially, this is true because different criteria sometimes obtain. In reality, however, it occurs because those who must decide have less of a feeling that society is being cheated.

Nurtured on the problem of hospital overcrowding, the concept of community psychiatry has developed to the point where the community is viewed as a sort of treatment setting. For many patients, this is a euphemistic acknowledgment of the fact that little effective treatment is available within the institution. In any event, unless a defendant who is found unfit to proceed with his trial is sent to an institution for the criminally insane, a disposition frequently reserved only for cases involving serious charges, he may be sent to an open door civil hospital where the community treatment notion prevails. Since he is handled there like other patients, the idea is to return him to the community as soon as possible, not in order to stand trial but for treatment. In New York, this defendant may then be back on the streets in a matter of hours after his arrival at the hospital. It is possible, thereby, for him to escape trial altogether while remaining at large in the community indefinitely.

Strangely enough, this tactic does not seem to be widely used by lawyers in the lesser cases we have been talking about. Instead, the bargain and plea tack which has already been discussed remains the one to which resort is most frequently had. Certainly, a number of lawyers may not yet be fully conversant with the likelihood of freedom for their clients that is implicit in the community treatment idea. Nevertheless, to my mind, that they do not make greater use of this device also represents a self-policing balance. Feelings of lawyers, as citizens themselves in and of the middle class, play a considerable role in determining the useful limits of psychiatry in the court. This bears on Menninger's statement, referred to earlier, about "common knowledge and not scientific." It suggests that, even in an adversary system, the advocates themselves, supposedly partisan to their clients and supposed laymen in the mental health field, are nonetheless judgmental in determining their initial choice of tactics. They seem to be affected by considerations of possible and likely social consequences at the floodgate stage, that is, in the process of deciding whether or not to permit mental health criteria to come into play. They also decide, for and on behalf of their clients, whether the mental health game is worth the candle based, in part, on the penal options and alternatives available. There is little doubt in my mind that more people would be adjudicated mentally ill or incompetent to stand trial if lower criminal court defendants were all rich and, at the same time, misdemeanor penalties were increased threefold.

It may seem that mental health personnel are mostly manipulated by the law and lawyers, used on their own terms to a certain extent, after being invited in, but then also criticized for not being another kind of animal. This is probably the reciprocal of feelings that many lawyers have to the effect that psychiatrists want their own formulations to displace the judgmental and dispositive role that society gives the judge and representatives of the general public.

I do not pretend to hold the key that will unlock this distrust and suspicion that seems to obtain between lawyers and psychiatrists. In the first place, I am not at all sure that less conflict and a firmer alliance is necessarily the goal. The coercive power of law, that is, of government, effectively combined with the ability of mental health to exercise control over human behavior, especially as this ability is enhanced by the use of drugs, would not be an unmixed blessing. Given the facts that law presently does not serve or represent all citizens equally and that psychiatry is now only one small part science, I doubt that if the two were more hand in glove than they are, the results would inevitably benefit either the average layman or those to whom we refer as mentally disordered offenders. A certain amount of constant tension leads to confusion of the sort we now experience. But if confusion and tension are perhaps built in, they nonetheless play a constructive role by leading to new procedures in law and new formulations in psychiatry. Procedures that are worked out in the court forum then undergo legislative and appellate scrutiny, for what these are worth. The necessity to reformulate requires that psychiatrists maintain closer touch with social conditions than they might do otherwise.

On this point we might consider the following words about psychiatry—in another country—from a recent editorial in *The New York Times*. "The misuse of psychiatric personnel and institutions to incarcerate political heretics has a long history in Russia. It is one of the instruments open to a totalitarian regime with a medical system in which the loyalty of physicians belongs primarily to their governmental employer rather than to their patients."

In the second place, I do not believe that we can arrive at a civilized and consistent forensic psychiatry or, if you will, a medically sensitive jurisprudence, just by creating interdisciplinary and cross professional cooperation. The real condition precedent is a more sophisticated understanding by the lay public of its need to be gratified and satisfied by the performance of both psychiatry and law, and a more realistic appreciation by it of the limitations of both professions in deterring and correcting. So long as the common social conditions that cause and underlie crime and mental illness continue unchecked, this understanding and appreciation cannot be expected. To mention just one statistic, we know that approximately 80 percent of mental illness is found among 10 percent of the population in the lowest economic stratum. It is surely important to go on treating everyone who needs treatment, but with a percentage figure like this, it is also possible to interpret psychiatric activity in the courts as a rhetorical balm for the middle class, something that puts off the day of reckoning for indifference and inactivity. The point that I am making is merely that forensic psychiatry is part and parcel of the whole legal apparatus. It is not sufficient, in order to legitimately disclaim responsibility for the overall oppressive effect of the criminal law structure, simply to have kept one's nose clean by honestly and sincerely grinding out the fairest psychiatric judgments of which one is capable, if the net effect of these efforts is to perpetuate present inequities and forestall essential changes in the larger framework system.

I should, nevertheless, like to offer two suggestions that seem to derive from what has gone before. One may appear trivial, but I will attempt to explain why it is important. The other may seem outrageous, but I will attempt to explain why it is realistic.

My first suggestion has to do with that most common of written communications between a psychiatrist and a judge or lawyer, the medicolegal report. Traditionally, this comes in three parts: a history at the beginning; an account of the examination, observations, treatment, and tests given; and, finally, the diagnosis, prognosis, and conclusions. An occasional author fearlessly adds a fourth section, presenting his own opinions about the sort of handling or treatment that seems indicated for the patient. However, most have become sensitive to charges that they are trying to usurp the responsibility of lawfully constituted judicial authority, or to overstep the bounds of their profession, and consequently, generally omit these opinions altogether or else insert them as innuendoes somewhere among the other sections.

The link that is missing from this format would be the most useful for the law, namely the "How come?" of the report. The big labelling words that Judge David Bazelon deplored are not nearly as important for an intelligent evaluation of mental condition as is the underlying explanatory reasoning that should, with reasonable medical certainty, connect the psychiatric observations with, for example, the diagnosis. How does this diagnosis actually explain the behavior that is the subject of the lawsuit? Exactly why do the test results and behavioral observations lead to and support the prognosis? Why, for example, does it follow, either logically or medically, that so-and-so is almost a sure bet to commit future violent assaults merely because he experienced certain events in his childhood or recently committed one such assault? What is the reason one inference is compelled, from the facts, to the effect that a defendant does or does not fit into a formulation of legal insanity?

The law stands in great need of a comprehensible explication of every psychiatric conclusion in each case, one that starts with verifiable data and that will permit others to make an informed evaluation of frequently conflicting professional judgments. Without this, psychiatrists are not helpful except as a cover story. The jury then has no choice but to flounder, to decide the case as a battle of medical pedigrees, or else merely to do instinctively what it damn well pleases.

Assuming the pedigrees to be approximately equal, this is what most frequently occurs, thereby resulting sometimes in both legal injustices and that social stability we have already mentioned which derives from having a mechanism to determine and rationalize the limits of tolerable overt deviance. This state of affairs psychiatrists themselves might be able to modify without causing undue chaos if they will offer the judge and jury a great deal more connecting matter leading to their conclusions than is now usual. In this way, conflicting testimony could be evaluated on its merits.

My second suggestion harkens back to the plaint of many psychiatrists that, although they themselves do not feel expert in certain areas about which they testify, it is operatives of the legal system which force them to act as such. "After all, what would we be doing in court in the first place," they ask, "if lawyers didn't want us there and the judge hadn't qualified us as experts?" They argue that if the legal profession invented psychiatric expertise on so many subjects, then it should learn to live with the consequences. They cite lawyer hypocrisy that permits counsel to be tongue in cheek when talking to psychiatrists privately one moment and pretending to be morally indignant and righteous when in court the next. "Why," they ask, "do lawyers go around saying all those bad things about us?"

It is not to exculpate the legal profession entirely to mention that there are counter arguments or formulations sometimes raised by lawyers. The reciprocal of these complaints may be heard in the locker rooms of court. What lawyers say about psychiatrists goes something like this. "Why do these guys weasel so much about the very things that they make their living deciding every day? Who else have we got to say these words? Isn't this supposed to be their bag?"

Lawyers would, indeed, be happier if psychiatrists never took the stand against their clients. Psychiatrists would be happier if they weren't grilled in public about how they make their judgments. Since both groups earn their living by being part of the system, and since psychiatrists, more than many like to realize, as well as lawyers, deal in value-loaded judgments, things would be easier if a pragmatic approach were adopted.

This implies that psychiatrists should accept at face value the favored, from the viewpoint of influencing others, status that this system offers them as experts. Another alternative is that they take steps to extricate themselves from the system altogether or to minimize their role in it, steps I suspect the profession as a whole would not endorse. Between M'Naghten and Freud there were no psychiatrists, yet legal decisions based on appraisals of mental state were made. Instead of publicly disavowing claims to expertise and saying they are in court only at the insistence of lawers and judges, they might do better by utilizing—manipulating or capitalizing on are the value words— the system in order to help achieve reforms and, in particular cases, those results that they believe should ensue.

This, of course, requires some change in the psychiatrist's self-image. It implies his willingness to consider himself and act as an opportunist of sorts during particular stages of the legal process in much the same way lawyers do at others. With a realistic view of his actual role in proceedings that function to officially dispose of individual offenders and issues of social conflict, the psychiatrist can more consciously, directly, and effectively work toward results he considers desirable.

As much as most lawyers, he is familiar with the facts of life behind whatever options the law affords an accused or a person whose civil cause depends on a ruling about past or present mental condition. The psychiatrist also knows and understands the consequences of his act of testifying and that his testimony is offered for the purpose of permitting society to make an official characterization that will have specific results for the person about whom his pronouncements are rendered. He can be on one or the other side in a case, but cannot really be objective or neutral; he can only pretend to believe that he is. Pretending puts him on the third side in every bilateral case, that of the system as it presently functions. If, then, the law casts him in the role of partisan in objective clothing, there seems little point in a psychiatrist's mistaking reality for the role, in playing coy by denying responsibility for the personal and social consequences that his pronouncements, if they are accepted, will invoke. This is the difference between rendering a psychiatric opinion in a hospital and rendering it in court.

A psychiatrist may modestly assert, for example, that he is no expert on the subject of a woman's fitness as a mother. He may consider such a judgment as properly being made by a panel of mothers. Or, he may believe that the question of whether or not a defendant has the mental capacity to aid in his own defense is a conclusion that should be drawn by that defendant's own lawyer or a panel of experienced and impartial defense lawyers convened for the purpose. Still, on matters of emotion, state of mind, or mental capacity, he is called to the stand, qualified as an expert, then asked his opinion about the mother's fitness or the defendant's capacity to understand the proceedings and participate in his own defense.

Of course, he may have no opinion. Or, he may testify that he has only a layman's opinion on these matters. But in either eventuality, that is, when in a matter of speaking he defaults, one of his colleagues will surely be found willing to come forward with the required opinion based on expertise.

Rather than do a soft shoe shuffle with his conscience about the realm of his real expertise, where he does have an opinion as to the best disposition of a particular case and also one, expert or not, about the matter in issue, the psychiatrist would do well not to abdicate. He should make use of his power and elect to assert his opinion, consciously clothed in the kind of language that will safeguard his favored status as an expert in the courtroom.

I suggest that, as the law operates at present, he should do this in order to achieve the results that he considers salutory.

REFERENCE

Lobenthal, Joseph S., Jr.: *Power and Put-on: The Law in America.* New York, Outerbridge & Dienstfrey, 1971.

Chapter 6

SYSTEMS APPROACH TO A CORRECTIONAL INSTITUTION

MAXWELL JONES AND MARGARET WEEKS

The concept of the therapeutic culture as applied to the socio-path originated with Dr. Maxwell Jones in his work in England. It was primarily those efforts which began his long history of influence on treatment processes as applied to the hospitalized patient. Through his work, he has become highly sensitized to the social system which operates in an institutional setting, skilled in the utilization of that system, and aware of the relevant parameters necessary to change that system. In his paper, he and Mrs. Margaret Weeks address themselves to some of the components of the systems which operate in a correctional setting as well as the variables which are important and necessary in trying to change our traditional correctional model.

EDITORS

From birth, we are all associated with varying kinds of social systems. A social system simply means a consistent social interaction with varying numbers of people over significant periods of time. Thus, the infant has a form of social system with the breast and with the mother during its first few months of life. This social system can widen to include the whole family and, later, outside persons who are contacted frequently. You all know the significance of the school social system and the social systems which develop around play, religion, etc. If a system fails to satisfy or leads to frustration, then a new social system may be sought or created, such as a deviant or delinquent gang. Such a deviant system then operates against the more orthodox social organization. Each social system has its own values and in deviant systems these will, by definition, be at variance with the ordinary norms of society. The development of a value system or culture is fraught with all kinds of difficulties. Take, for example, the relationship between parents and a young child. It is relatively easy to condone the behavior of a child of two because no ordinary person doubts that the child is not responsible for most of his actions. The child tends to take and eat that which attracts his attention, knock down and wound his rival sibling, play with fire, expose his genitals, etc. This behavior, although understood, is only marginally sanctioned, and sanctions are seldom consistently applied. The performance and attitudes of parents in rearing their children vary from day to day. Many other factors come into the picture. For example, most parents are very conscious of the expectations of child behavior in their neighborhood. They tend to mirror what they recall of their own parents' expectations in this respect or to do the opposite. The main difficulty arises, however, over the question of punishment. What harassed mother has not felt the sting of conscience when slapping her overdemanding or anxiety-provoking offspring. Even in a setting of emotional calm, the rational application of force in a conscious attempt to teach the child the difference between right and wrong creates a difficult interaction between mother and child and raises doubts, at least momentarily, as to the validity of this method of teaching. The interaction between the child and adult is difficult enough even in bringing up children in an ordinary family. The quality of these relationships will largely determine the future personality of the child. When the parents are absent, uninterested, or actively rejecting, the result may be a severe character disorder developing in the child.

In considering social systems, values, attitudes, and beliefs, we are entering the vague and confusing field of culture. A culture means the attitudes and beliefs which are internalized in individuals and which, to a large extent, determine the roles and role relationships within any social system. These problems assume a national scale when one considers the present state of the United States and many other countries. Hippies represent a new and constantly changing series of systems, with very divergent types of culture depending on their socioeconomic background and other variables. In *The Greening of America*, Charles Reich (1970) attempted to capture something of the process of change occurring within the United States. Many critics think that he tended to generalize from the more privileged students at

Yale University, who represented a social system or culture which had little to do with similar groups in underprivileged areas. Author Reich's "Consciousness III" represents an end product of a revolution in thought against the current value system of a competitive, materialistic, and success-oriented value system, which he epitomized with the term "the corporate state." It seems to me that the importance of Reich's book is to bring out the possibility of change within a social system, which can represent a new value system based on individual rights, an overall sharing of the good things in life, and a deep feeling of responsibility for others.

One of our experiences (M.J.'s, 1947–1959) in the Social Rehabilitation Unit at Belmont Hospital, near London, which was later renamed Henderson Hospital, clearly demonstrated the importance of values and a social system which represented a therapeutic culture.

Henderson Hospital was an early example of a model for change in the direction of a therapeutic culture. There were a hundred beds for cases of psychopathy, mainly referred from the courts. These young people could readily have been sent to prison, but an insightful judge thought that punishment would be less appropriate than some attempt at changing antisocial attitudes and helping their emotional growth. It is the authors' belief that social systems of this kind should become more prevalent within the overall prison system. Although the parallel is not too close, as for instance the fact that Henderson Hospital had both male and female patients, the model still holds as at least an example of a change system. One could reasonably ask whether it really is harmful to mix male and female prisoners? Could one afford to have female custodial staff as well as male? Such a practice is common in disturbed psychiatric wards with many court referrals, and it is now well accepted within the medical profession that female nurses may have many attributes lacking in a totally male nurse population. This, however, has not always been the situation. In the early 1940's, when moving female nurses and attendants onto male wards was a beginning experiment, it was met with loud cries of protest and catastrophic predictions. The general reaction from laymen was that females would be attacked. This attitude reflected the overall assumption that prisoners were bad people who did bad things. These reactions may have been largely or partially true, but what we are now trying to emphasize is that such attitudes and beliefs need to be reconsidered. For instance, the same logic would apply in the disturbed psychiatric ward where female nurses are as exposed to such potential danger as they would be in a prison system.

The issue, also, of whether or not punishment has a deterrent effect on the prisoner is one still in great debate and again our emphasis is directed toward alleviating the dehumanizing processes which exist in many penal institutions. Maintaining some of the inhumane conditions may reflect some of our own aggressive, punitive hostility toward the criminal. Belief in a rehabilitative process, instead, is still not generally prevalent in our society or, at the best, we experience great ambivalence in our convictions about the return of the criminal to society.

At Henderson Hospital, the various attitudes and beliefs were examined and, as far as possible, a value system was established based on the realities of the situation rather than on prejudice and misunderstanding. In order to do this, it was decided that it would be made clear to the patients that the staff was not absolutely certain how the staff could help them to change in the direction of greater social acceptance. From the start, it was made quite clear that the role relationship of staff and patients was one of mutual interaction with a view to learning, being able to empathize with their particular problems, and social and cultural difficulties. Thus, by diminishing the social distance between staff and patients, a process was initiated which was eventually to lead to relatively good two-way communication, shared decision making, and learning as a social process. These concepts seem worthwhile to enumerate in the hope that they may be acceptable as a possible model for change within the prison system.

THE AUTHORITY SYSTEM

The warden and senior staff in any prison system has a tremendous responsibility, and yet it can be reasonably compared with the authority structure in schools and various types of institutions, which may in their own way have equal responsibility. The important thing about an authority system is that it should be as close as possible to the people for whom the system is responsible. The question of trust hangs like a cloud over such systems. Thus, the warden and his senior staff may have liberal ideas, but they are responsible to the state, and the legislature often has relatively less knowledge and understanding of the problem for which the prison staff is responsible. In such a situation, even a liberal warden may, through his need to conform to higher authority, appear as repressive and even cruel, when, in fact, given a free choice, he would choose to do otherwise.

Similar problems in terms of responsibility, attitudes, and freedom of choice bedevil the relations between custodial personnel and prisoners. A close relationship between prison personnel and prisoners may be frowned upon by the authorities and make close relationships impossible. Another common factor is the old guard who frequently views with suspicion the changing attitudes of the more liberal kind, which are now prevalent in all social systems. To change such a system requires a great deal of courage on the part of top administration. This kind of change is always viewed with suspicion and fear because it affects the life of individuals within the system. However, sanctions from above in the form of a positive liberal attitude by the warden can expedite the process of change. One of the authors (M.J.) has had an experience with a group of this kind. As the group started to interact in some formal planned way, the more resistant old guard became curious and at least wanted to know more about what was happening. In other words, a model is established and this model may serve as a point of departure for discussion and even education within the most resistant subgroup within the prison system.

It seems to us that only when the authority system at the top is able to look at its attitudes and discuss relationships at a "gut level," can one then feel that personnel are in a position to discuss similar topics with the prisoners. The degree of responsibility and authority which can be delegated to prisoners clearly varies with the nature of the prison and the sophistication of the correctional personnel. Current events are forcing us to realize the similarity between this dilemma and the dilemma within the whole of our society, whether it be on the college campus, in the elementary school, in the home, and most significant of all, within the political system.

TWO-WAY COMMUNICATION

What has been said about the authority system applies directly to two-way communication. In the meetings of top administration, and at other levels within the prison, discussion about the whole system should take place. These discussions, to be effective, require a degree of trust which allows free discussion of feelings and disagreement at all levels. Such disagreements properly handled can lead to learning because the examination of varying points of view is one way in which learning as a social process is invoked. Risk taking is implicit in such interaction and if some junior within the group risks expressing critical ideas about the whole system and particularly about the leadership, then this must be seen as a positive form of criticism, which may lead to change in attitudes rather than for it to be negated and even punished. To encourage communication, one must have security and the knowledge that no reprisals will be taken, even if the attitudes expressed are very different from those of the power structure. Again, the same argument applies at all levels within the system and the interaction between the custody personnel and the prisoners has to aim at some such freedom to communicate without fear of reprisal.

SHARED DECISION MAKING

Communication systems of the kind that we have described inevitably moves us in the direction of shared decision making. An obvious generalization is that if a plan is to be tried, it is more likely to succeed if all the people who will participate in the actual carrying out of the plan have been in on the planning process. Even at the lowest level and yet the most important of the system.

For example, if the prisoners take on responsibility for certain aspects of discipline within the living unit, then the motivation to change is greatly heightened. Ultimately, one is concerned with the lives of prisoners, with a view to helping them to become part of society outside, and this kind of responsibility is an essential part of a learning experience in terms of shared responsibility.

SOCIAL LEARNING

We would like to start with the basic assumption that teaching and learning are complementary. One can, we think, make a somewhat arbitrary distinction between teaching or the acquisition of knowledge by a process of one-way communication and learning as a subjective experience involving two-way communication and some modification of the personality. In this sense, teaching implies that the student is the passive recipient of information and has no opportunity to interact with the teacher with a view to exploring the subject being taught. Learning is a social process. We use the term "social learning" to describe the interactional process motivated by some inner need or stress that leads to the overt expression of feeling involving cognitive processes and learning. There appears to be the need for instruction by the generally accepted teaching methods to passive recipients. At the other end of the spectrum, if growth is to occur, far more attention than at present will have to be paid to some process like social learning.

One of the authors (M.J.) views teaching as generally far too impersonal. He agrees with Eric Erickson and many others that maturation and learning are frequently associated with times of crisis which call for some immediate resolution if the tension is to be relieved. In such settings, the individual is highly motivated to learn and the presence of a skilled teacher, familiar with group dynamics, can hasten this process. Discussion of interpersonal problems must arouse feeling, whether it is expressed overtly or covertly. Frequently, individuals tend to cover up their feelings and such tendencies are encouraged in our culture. Moreover, feelings are frequently repressed and unconscious. It may take considerable skill on the part of the prison group leader to create a group climate in which such latent feelings may become manifest.

People often lack the motivation to examine their feelings, let alone share them with others. In our competitive and insecure world, it is hard to find a group climate where there is a sense of security without fear of reprisal. To achieve such a group climate requires a social structure where the sanctions are positive and there is no threat from the abuse of authority. Such a climate is difficult to achieve in a therapeutic group and even more so in staff meetings, training programs, family groups, or situations in a prison. In other words, the social milieu in which social learning can occur is as important as the skills required to analyze interpersonal interactions within a group, to uncover latent content, and to examine the various solutions to problems raised in such a group. Social learning is used to cover this set of circumstances and the terms "living-learning situation" and "crisis situation" are used in a very arbitrary way to refer mainly to the amount of feeling inherent in the situation. When there is a moderate degree of anxiety, as occurs in most interpersonal interactions around problems of everyday living, whether in hospital or in prison, we use the term "living-learning situation." Where, however, there is severe anxiety, the term "crisis situation" is used.

In both "crisis situations" and "living-learning situations," the term "confrontation" is used to convey the bringing together of involved individuals, which makes social interaction, the expression of feeling, and social learning possible (Jones and Polak, 1968). The confrontation may or may not succeed in its purpose of resolving a conflict or achieving a learning situation. The outcome of the confrontation depends on the inherent skills of the participants, the motivation of the individuals concerned, the nature and complexity of the conflict or crisis and, above all, an objective teacher with psychodynamic skills. The timing of the confrontation is of extreme importance, particularly in a crisis.

If unduly delayed, it may lead to disaster and the opportunity of creating a social learning situation may be lost. Even in living-learning situations, confrontation should occur at the time when the interaction is in progress. To talk about a situation retrospectively deprives it of much of its feeling tone, which seems to be an essential ingredient in social learning. It is for this reason that much of the supervision that occurs in formal training may be less effective than it would if the supervisor were a participant in the ongoing living-learning situation or crisis.

SUMMARY

An attempt to outline a systems approach to change in a correctional system has been attempted. To many, it will appear glib and unrealistic. Such a program takes several years to implement and requires leadership and staff, both of whom must be dedicated and motivated to change. Only then can the interest and power of the peer group of prisoners complement the skills of the staff. The general principles regarding change discussed here are relevant to all forms of social institution, whether prison, hospital, school, or local community (Jones, 1968a, 1968b).

REFERENCES

Jones, Maxwell: *Beyond the Therapeutic Community.* New Haven, Yale, 1968a.
Jones, Maxwell: *Social Psychiatry in Action.* Baltimore. Penguin, 1968b.
Jones, Maxwell and Polak, Paul: Crisis and confrontation. *Br J Psychiatr,* 114:169, 1968.
Reich, Charles A.: *The Greening of America.* New York, Random, 1970.

Chapter 7

CAMPUS PRISONS, COMMUNITY PRISONS, AND JUDICIAL ADMINISTRATION

NORMAN I. BARR AND LEONARD ZUNIN

Drs. Norman Barr and Leonard Zunin are very persuasive in asking us to change the traditional and unsuccessful approaches to handling the convicted individual. Indeed, they suggest that unless changes are made, the chances are good for our American culture to be torn asunder from within. One concept they propose, that of community-based prisons, has been generally accepted by our correctional systems. The other two concepts are both innovative and provocative. The first of these, locating prisons on university campuses, is particularly compelling in view of the advantages the authors believe would accrue to the problems of corrections. Secondly, they propose that the administration of our correctional system be taken from the executive branch of government and given to the judiciary. They point out that historical precedent rather than planning placed corrections within the executive branch of government. It is their contention that the purposes and goals of corrections can be better served by the judiciary.

EDITORS

Gaining Public Support

The weakest link in the chain of any society is the people in that society who are locked up involuntarily. The strength of every society can be measured by whom it incarcerates.

In a tyranny or closed society, we find in its prisons people who oppose the tyrant, his authoritarian philosophy, and lack of freedom and justice. In a democratic or open society, we anticipate that prisons house discordant individuals whose crimes are inacted singularly. The prison population in a tyranny reflects disproportionate percentages of the groups of citizens who are tyrannized. The prison population of an open democracy is expected to reflect a genuine cross section of the total population.

The American society is in trouble. Evidence for this can be found in every prison, jail, and courtroom across the land. Amer-

ica's most important product, like any government's, is people—
and it is failing them. American Corrections has jurisdiction on
any given day of 1¼ million people, one of every 160 Americans.
Of these, 400,000 are incarcerated, the rest serving on parole or
probation. These 1¼ million Americans include a disproportionate
abundance of poor people. A disproportionate abundance of
young people. A disproportionate abundance of Black people.
A disproportionate abundance of Spanish-speaking people. A disproportionate abundance of undereducated people.

If this country is to solve its correctional problems, it must
also find solutions to the causes of crime. The two are indivisible—
one and inseparable. To focus on one, ignoring the other, is to
misunderstand human nature—guaranteeing failure.

The challenge of corrections, and its importance, lies in its
central nature to the society. The American culture, for two
centuries having withstood valiantly all external pressures, can
succumb to internal force from its own people. The ignition
could occur at Kent State University or more likely at Attica
Prison. Considering that one of every 160 Americans is under
correctional jurisdiction, and if each of these has three close
relatives (parents, siblings, spouses, children), one of every 40
families is directly affected. This potentially potent force is
generally unrepresented and regularly unheard. However, it
grows impatient. It yells louder. It demands more—an equal
and fair share.

Correctional solutions are not novel. Among penologists, they
are widely known, largely agreed upon, and rarely put into effect.
Action rarely proceeds beyond the appointment of blue ribbon
commissions to study the problems and present solutions, which
they dutifully do, at large costs, and presenting the same solutions
that were not acted upon when the previous commission presented
them.

The most recent (1971) commission report in California rec-
ommended to Governor Ronald Reagan the abandonment of
Folsom and San Quentin Prisons because neither was secure or
safe. Other recommendations included conjugal visitations, wear-
ing of civilian clothes, background music at mealtime, modesty

toilet panels, individual cells, increased contact between inmates and staff, and emphasis on community involvement.

(N. B. recalls when, as Chief of Psychiatric Services for the Federal Bureau of Prisons in 1970, he was asked to prepare a report on how to improve the Medical Center for Federal Prisoners, Springfield, Missouri. He wrote, "Remove the inmates and blow the place up." Everyone agreed with the wisdom of his recommendation. None of them had the courage to light the dynamite. Not the dynamite to bring down the prison. Rather, the dynamite to awaken public opinion.)

Getting public support is the major problem which penologists have not solved. Once they do, other solutions will follow. Until they do, little meaningful progress can occur. If penologists do not ignite the dynamite soon, the inmates may. Inmates are unpredictable when handling dynamite.

As mentioned, we experienced penologists know all the solutions. Our literature over the past 20 years has supplied that. Numerous professional meetings have supplemented what gaps exist. There is little new to be gained by more communication amongst professionals regarding the already agreed upon solutions; except, perhaps, for us to reassure ourselves that we are the professionals. Otherwise, we might become indistinguishable from inmates—who are also professional penologists. They know the same solutions we do, only probably better.

There is much to be gained if we, as a single voice, can somehow speak out loud and clear enough to be heard by the public. This paper presents three alternative directions for corrections to move simultaneously in order to gain public support. The first and third directions, campus prisons and judicial administration, are relatively novel. The second direction, community prisons, is not new. Before discussing these, we will first develop historical perspective on prisons and prison programs.

Prison Development

Initially, the development of prisons as institutions began for the purpose of detaining a man while he awaited his punishment—

usually some combination of deprivation, torture, disfigurement, or death. Early prisons were owned by private individuals and were run for profit. It was originally understood that no prison should offer a standard of living higher than that of the very poorest free subjects, otherwise they would flock to fill the prisons. Wardenships were bought, bestowed, or inherited.

With the advent of the industrial revolution in the seventeenth century, prisons became excessively overcrowded. Direct governmental involvement was initiated by Great Britain which began the practice of transportation of inmates, mainly to the colonies of Virginia and the Carolinas. The American Revolution in 1776 forced Great Britain to switch to the use of old ships' hulks (publicly owned and essentially discarded) to provide living quarters for inmates. The architectural model for most large prisons today is a dubious American distinction and was first provided by the opening of Auburn Prison in New York with its congregate system in 1813. The silent system of solitary confinement, also an American contribution, was initiated at Cherry Hill Prison, Philadelphia, in 1829. Though never widely utilized, it had a very influential theoretical impact.

Selective Prisons

Selective prisons were first conceived by Plato who described three types: "One for persons charged with a crime, one for minor offenders and one for major criminals." The Spanish Inquisition also established three kinds of prisons: one for crimes of heresy, one for non-heresy crimes, and one for non-heresy crimes committed by employees of the Holy Office.

Maximum, Medium, and Minimum Security

In 1790, the hardened prisoners at the Old Walnut Street Jail in Philadelphia, the forerunner of Cherry Hill Prison, were placed in the "penitentiary house," the first known use of that term. Elmira Reformatory opened in upstate New York in 1876 as the world's first "reformatory," a prison for less serious offenders. The Rauhus Haus near Hamburg, Germany, in 1880, was the earliest "cottage system" prison breaking from the "silent" and "congregate" architectural systems. Lorton Reformatory, Washington, D.C., opened in 1915, as the first American cottage-style prison.

Prisons for Women

In 1593, in Amsterdam, Holland, the first prison for women only was established. It remained as the world's only such institution until 1780. The first American prison for women only was opened in Indiana in 1873.

Youth Institutions

In 1825, New York City opened the House of Refuge for boys and girls under the age of 20. Parkhurst, in 1839, became the first British prison exclusively for juvenile offenders.

Transportation

The biblical banishment of Adam and Eve from the Garden of Eden was transformed by early correctional philosophy to banishment of a convicted offender to a remote mine, quarry, or assignment to a galley ship. British banished prisoners via transportation to the American Colonies from 1619 to 1776, and to Australia from 1787 to 1867. The construction of the oldest American Federal Penitentiary, located on McNeil Island off the coast of Washington, and the most secure American federal penitentiary, Alcatraz (now unused) on "the rock" in San Francisco Bay, were forms of transportation. When the Federal Penitentiary on McNeil Island was opened in 1867, transferring a prisoner there from Mississippi or Massachusetts was equivalent to banishing him from the Garden of Eden.

PROGRAM DEVELOPMENT

Humane Rehabilitation

The concept of rehabilitation originated when the Justinian Code in the first century declared it illegal to punish a man who was already imprisoned and further stated that the purpose of prison was solely to detain him. In sixteenth century Renaissance Italy (Lombroso), the criminal was considered to be someone needing treatment until he conformed to the social standards of his time and place. The early seventeenth century Bridewell Prison in Amsterdam, Holland was the first prison to provide medical care, religious services, and classes in reading, writing, and arithmetic for inmates. By the late eighteenth century, the notable prison reformer, John Howard, assisted the British Parliament in enacting a law ordering "whitewashing of walls and ceilings once a year, cleaning and ventilation of rooms, clothing for the naked and as little use as possible of the underground dungeons."

In the early nineteenth century, inmates' wives were first allowed to visit them once every three months. At this time, the second great prison reformer, Elizabeth Fry, pushed for classification of all inmates by age, sex, and offense. The 1823 Gaol Act in Britain stated that if a prisoner could not have his own cell then, at least, he should have his own bed. In 1840, Maconachie in Australia, followed in 1853 by Crofton in Ireland, innovated work release programs, as well as parole during the last year of a man's sentence. Massachusetts developed probation for juveniles in the 1870's, and the Catholic Priest, Father Cook of Boston, became the world's first probation officer.

Indeterminate Sentencing

Indeterminate sentencing was innovated by Charles V in 1530, when he ordered imprisonment of convicted offenders if there was good reason to expect future crimes unless someone paid a sufficient security to indemnify future victims. Benjamin Rush, Father of American Psychiatry, advocated remission of part of a sentence for hard labor and good behavior in 1757. Thirty years later, John Howard sought long sentences with intended reductions for inmate's amendments. The Bavarian Code (1813) was the first legislative attempt to establish minimum and maximum sentences for all inmates. Twenty-seven years later, Maconachie developed the mark system, whereby a fixed number of marks earned by the inmate resulted in the termination of his sentence. Spanish prisoners in the mid-1800's could earn up to one-half of their sentence. The first indeterminate sentence law in the United States was enacted by New York State in 1897.

Inmate Labor

Prison industries, or work for inmates, had its early beginnings in the sixteenth century in Bridewell Prison, where inmates received a small wage for goods they produced. In 1627, the Maison de Force, in Austria, provided work for all inmates. In 1703, at the Hospice of St. Michel in Rome, prisoners spun and knitted with one leg chained to a bench while the priest read pious works to them aloud. In the early eighteenth century, the unfortunate development of idle labor such as the crank, the treadmill, and stone-breaking began. Useful training for several trades was initiated in 1773 in Ghent, Austria, and prisoners who worked were allowed to retain one-half of their wages. By the 1790's, prisoners in Philadelphia's Walnut Street Jail retained part of their profits. Elizabeth Fry, in 1818, argued before Parliament for fair wages to all inmates.

Current Penology

Today, American prisons include about 400 institutions for adult felons, ranging from forestry camps to some of the world's largest and oldest prisons. Twenty-one of these prisons house over 2,000 men and four (in California, Illinois, Michigan, and Ohio) house 4,000 inmates. The concept of banishment in the sense of placement in remote areas is still prominent. On the positive side, there have been numerous significant advances in prison programming during the past decade.

CAMPUS PRISONS

Regarding the need for penology to influence public opinion in order to gain its support, there are three primary areas for evolutionary development. The first of these is the building of prisons on university campuses. American universities, as centers of knowledge, have solved problems ranging from the development of the atomic bomb to landing men on the moon. Corrections and academia, however, have always maintained a cool relationship with each other even though some of the largest American universities are located in the same states with the largest prisons.

The next 50 prisons constructed in the United States should be located on university campuses, one in each state. Not located off-campus or just beyond the city limits, but next to the law school, the medical school, the social sciences building, and chapel.

This development would educate the public to the fact that solving correctional problems, including improving law enforcement, crime control techniques, and understanding the relationship between criminal behavior and social policy, is in its own best interest. It would communicate to the inmates that they have not been forgotten or banished and that the society to which they feel alien, is committed and dedicated to helping them. Campus prisons would facilitate the taking of university courses by inmates.

Campus prisons would also provide an opportunity to expand the professional manpower pool in corrections. Undergraduate students might take a course in criminology or sociology given inside the prison. If enough students took these courses, then more students might be encouraged to major in corrections and related helping fields and to devote their professional lives to this end. Opportunities for graduate studies and for research in corrections would be enhanced. Graduate students in related fields like theology, psychology, medicine, and law could work and learn in prisons. A sad commentary on the current status of correctional manpower is the paucity of contacts with prisons experienced by most practicing doctors, ministers, sociologists, psychiatrists, psychologists, lawyers, and even judges.

Even the college student who never goes within the prison perimeter would see the prison every day and learn to understand that it is a place for housing unhappy human beings rather than vile, evil, malicious, perverted, syphilitic, atheistic, communistic, and militant convicts. After graduation, he would return to his community and, hopefully, share this knowledge with his fellow citizens.

A historical precedent for the development of prisons on campus is the building of mental hospitals on campus. Formerly, old insane asylums matched prisons in architectural obsolescence and geographic inaccessibility. Recent construction of mental hospitals on many university campuses, however, has been a major factor in developing better methods for treating the mentally ill.

COMMUNITY PRISONS

The second evolutionary development, the community prison concept, is described in the report of the 1967 Presidential Task Force on Corrections. This concept involves the building of multiple, small correctional facilities located in communities from which the inmate population originates and helps dissolve the we–them dichotomy (the good guys vs the bad guys) which otherwise naturally develops. It includes the use of available community facilities, employment of community personnel, and flexibility for alternatives like half-way houses. Emphasis is on personal contact between staff and inmates and the human, whole man approach. The distinction between correctional officer and probation officer is dissolved because the same staff person maintains contact with the inmate whether he is paroled into the community or incarcerated in the community center.

Management of work release; study release; weekend, night-time, or daytime detention; parole; reincarceration; conjugal visitations; and contact with family and friends become important aspects of the inmate's personal rehabilitation. Where treatment or therapy is involved, the principles and practices of reality therapy as described by Dr. William Glasser are most useful.

A beneficial and much-needed result of community prisons would be the employment of local citizens. A major problem in corrections today results because inmates tend to be poor, minority, radical, and urban. Whereas, prison personnel are largely middle-class, majority, conservative, and rural. Corrections needs a large influx of Black personnel at all levels, especially upper management. Recent isolated appointments of Black wardens is a step in the right direction. However, if these assignments are not made on a large scale, then they will degenerate into isolated and meaningless acts of "Uncle Tomism."

The Federal Bureau of Prisons approaches the community prisons concept through its community treatment centers (CTC). First established in 1961, there are now nine CTC in operation. These centers have a bed capacity for 300 men and were originally designed as halfway-out houses. Inmates approaching parole could use them for the last 60 days of their sentence. Federal prisoners are currently processed through the CTC at a rate of 1500 men per year, plus an additional 500 men who go to other halfway facilities with which the Federal Government has contractual agreements. Legislation passed by Congress at the end of 1970 also allows the CTC to be used by federal probationers and parolees as halfway-in houses. During the first six months of this new law, 55 men were admitted to the CTC by this route. Considering that the present federal inmate population is 21,000 men, the community program is still relatively small. However, it is a potential waking giant.

JUDICIAL ADMINISTRATION

The third evolutionary direction is the increasing participation of the Judiciary. Chief Justice Warren Burger has taken a particularly active role in guaranteeing the rights of convicted offenders. This judicial responsibility is appropriate since it is the court which declares a man guilty and sends him to prison. We may then ask when is an offender no longer guilty, and who should make this decision? Does guilt end when he is paroled? When he is pardoned? At the conclusion of his sentence? When he is eligible again to vote and run for public office? Or never? Does the court's responsibility to an inmate terminate at the conclusion of the trial? Of the appeal? Of the sentence? If the court's responsibility extends to the end of the sentence, then it should exercise a continuing responsibility, an administrative role in corrections.

Our premise, then, is that the Judicial, rather than the Executive Branch of government, should be responsible for the administration of corrections.

The executive branch of government currently administers corrections as a result of historical prison development. When prison management changed from private to public control, the executive branch naturally assumed this responsibility. Modern society and penology can no longer tolerate this aberrant development. The executive branch of government in a free society is responsive to political pressures. This is incompatible with sound prison management because public opinion is often frivolous and contrary to good penal practice. While judicial administration would not encourage popular support, it would eliminate the negative aspects or the lack of it by decreasing political considerations in the development of sound prison programming.

The courts necessarily inherit the administrative role in corrections because they, like corrections, share a direct interest in the prevention of crime as well as the rehabilitation of offenders. The administration of corrections by the judicial branch would move politics further from prison management. (This would not be true where the judiciary is elected rather than appointed.) The historic precedent for the court's assuming responsibility for administering prisons occurred in 1940, when the Federal Bureau of Prisons relinquished supervision of the Probation Service to the Administrative Office of the United States Supreme Court. For the past 31 years, federal corrections has been administered by the executive branch of government. Whereas, federal parole and probation has been administered by the judicial branch. Should the probation service remain under the court's leadership, or should it be returned to the executive branch to be administratively reunited with corrections? To this frequently debated question, we offer another alternative, namely, to reunite corrections with probation by transferring the Bureau of Prisons to the Administrative Office of the Supreme Court. Reunification of corrections with probation is essential for implementing the previously described community concept of relating to the offender as a human, whole man. The reunion, therefore, should take place within the judicial rather than the executive branch.

SUMMARY

In conclusion, the major task facing penologists today is to gain broad public support for widely agreed upon solutions. We offer three directions for evolutionary development in order to achieve this end. These are the development of campus prisons, the expanded utilization of the community prisons concept, and the assumption of administrative responsibility for corrections by the judiciary.

Chapter 8

CURRENT RESEARCH IN DRUGS AND BEHAVIOR AS IT RELATES TO THE MENTALLY DISORDERED OFFENDER

Albert Weissman

The development and use of psychotropic medications has been one of the most significant occurrences within the mental health field in several decades. Their use with a patient population has been widely documented. However, their specific application and effectiveness with the mentally disordered offender has received very little attention. Dr. Albert Weissman has addressed himself to this special population and presented information about the specific problems, utility, and considerations relevant to a mentally disordered offender population. In as much as medications are widely used with this population, the need for such a paper is considerable.

Editors

Two extreme and diametrically opposed positions are often voiced by those who are not, in fact, responsible for developing drugs that exert beneficial effects on human behavior. First, there are drug nihilists, who see pharmacotherapy as an unnecessary, dangerous, and even immoral means of altering nervous function. This view is irrational. It ignores the fact that nervous function is modified continuously by endogenous chemicals, particularly neurotransmitters and neuromodulators that the body itself makes. There is now ample evidence in certain behavior disorders that the body's manufacture of these internal drugs and their metabolites is aberrant. It follows that there is no real means of isolating the brain and behavior from drugs, since drugs manufactured in the body make the brain go in the first place. Several lines of evidence indicate that important classes of drugs used in human psychopharmacology act by modifying this aberrant body chemistry.

Individuals who focus on hazards are also imbued with caution and conservatism in their attitudes towards drug research. The potential dangers of drugs, certain ethical considerations relative to drug research, and the fallout that can result from unfortunate incidents in man suggest to them a need for perfect safety in human research. Without minimizing the dangers of new therapies, even in the face of the exhaustive preparatory laboratory testing required by law, it should be recognized that requirements intended to guarantee absolute safety stifle progress. The dilemmas to be resolved in practical psychopharmacological research are how to weigh potential therapeutic benefit against the risks entailed and how to avoid the stagnation that can result from overcaution.

Secondly, there are those who assert that drugs that alter behavior can perform near miracles and even modify social progress by exerting specific actions on the behavior of key individuals. Kenneth Clark, President of the American Psychological Association, had expounded such a view as an article of faith. In his presidential address to the Association in 1971, he advocated and looked forward to the development of drugs that will reduce the aggressive behavior of world leaders. When they are developed, such drugs, according to Clark, will alleviate many of the world's problems.

The truth, as most individuals working in this area will agree, lies between these two extremes. From the advent of modern psychopharmacology in the early 1950's, until now, an impressive battery of drugs, acting reasonably specifically on human behavior, has been developed. Many of these drugs have unquestionable efficacy in treating various psychiatric patients. There is little basis, however, for believing that thought or political control by drugs is either an imminent hazard or a potential social boon.

The use of any therapy with mentally disordered offenders presents complex problems, but none more so than the use of drug therapy. Even though their illogical behavioral aberrations are not deterred by confinement or the threat of confinement, mentally disordered offenders are frequently rejected by medical institutions. Yet, with very few and as yet controversial exceptions, efforts to characterize mentally disordered offenders in terms of anatomical or physiological characteristics have failed.

The public seems unwilling to classify such individuals as either criminals or mentally ill. There is a clear challenge to employ and discover treatments which may be applicable on a large scale, rapid in action, and, above all, significantly effective. Drug therapy, when it exists, appears to be the most practical answer. In some instances, drug therapies for specific problems of the mentally disordered offender may already be in hand, although the lack of serious research directed towards this issue is clear. Who, as a prime example, has collected data on the effects of drugs on recidivism? In some instances, research towards appropriate drugs is proceeding. In all too many instances, however, there is no one, either in contact with mentally disordered offenders or in pharmacology laboratories, who is confronting the problem of the development of practical new therapies. Even where thought is being applied, the legal and administrative problems entailed in taking chances on truly novel drugs in man inhibits their development.

Perhaps, the *non plus ultra* of therapeutic behaviorally active drugs is antipsychotic medication. It is in this area that psychopharmacology has made its most impressive contributions. Those drugs in present use fall into one of three chemical categories, namely, the phenothiazines, such as chlorpromazine and trifluoperazine; the thioxanthenes, such as thiothixene; and the butyrophenones, of which the best-known representative is haloperidol. Certain of these drugs exert selective actions against severe thought disorder, mania, and, perhaps most relevant, paranoid hostility and aggressiveness. The newer agents in these classes are marked by a relative lack of sedative and cardiovascular activity.

Drugs in these classes are not equivalent. Darling (1971), for example, has reported that haloperidol is of particular value in violent, psychotic prisoners. Out of 30 chronically assaultive patients he studied at Massachusetts State Hospital, Bridgewater, 20 improved substantially on haloperidol after several phenothiazines had been tried and failed. Over a five-month period of observation, the patients were no longer assaultive, were substantially less psychotic, and engaged in some socialization or activity.

A second type of behavior drug of great importance is the antidepressants, such as imipramine, amitriptyline, and doxepin. The latter agent has been shown to combine antidepressant and antianxiety activity. These agents counteract severe endogenous and reactive depressions, and some studies suggest that suicide incidence in depressives is reduced. In the New York Prison System, the prototypical suicide victim can be characterized quite precisely. He is a newly confined, young, male narcotics addict. Along with other treatments and precautions, it seems to me that consideration could be given to the use of antidepressants in such subjects as a possible adjunctive means of reducing suicide frequency, although the relatively slow onset of action of these drugs presents a problem. Although the efficacy of antidepressant medications needs to be improved, there is also a pressing need for the development of equally efficacious antidepressant drugs with more rapid action than those currently available. It is important to stress that antidepressants of the type ordinarily used in therapy (the tricyclics) are not euphoriant and their abuse potential, in contrast to that of psychomotor stimulants such as amphetamine, is negligible.

A third class of behaviorally acting drugs well known in therapy is comprised of the antianxiety drugs, the so-called minor tranquilizers, chiefly the benzodiazepines such as chlordiazepoxide and diazepam. There are those who would discount the activity of such agents, since their record of safety has rendered them ubiquitous in our society. Nevertheless, this family of drugs has many pronounced actions which can be seen in laboratory animals and that probably translate to man. Their anticonvulsive and muscle relaxant activity are marked. However, some of their behavior actions in animals may be pertinent to mentally disordered offenders. For example, benzodiazepines in animals often markedly counteract aggressive and fighting behavior. On the other hand, under some circumstances, these drugs seem to free inhibited behavior, that is, they may enable an animal whose behavior is suppressed on account of the presentation of anxiety-evoking stimuli to behave more normally. Perhaps this loss of inhibition is the reason why, in man, benzodiazepines appear to be contraindicated in truly psychotic patients. Loss of behavioral inhibition is seldom, if ever, therapeutic in such patients.

Offenses committed by mentally disordered children should not escape our attention. The beneficial role that amphetamine and methylphenidate can play in modifying the hyperactivity of children with so-called minimal brain syndrome is a profound one, despite our failure to understand the condition. Considerable laboratory work is in progress to find animal models of hyperactivity in which amphetamine can be shown to exert a depressant effect instead of its customary stimulation. The development of such models could pave the way for the discovery of improved agents for hyperkinetic children, although in this area widespread concern that safety be absolute and paramount is anything but conducive for clinical testing of such discoveries in affected children. There is no hard evidence that children who are medicated with amphetamine or similar drugs come to abuse these drugs more than their unaffected cohorts as they mature. Pharmacologists do not understand the mechanism whereby stimulant drugs, so commonly abused in older youths and adults, should exert dramatic beneficial effects in pathologically hyperactive young children. The evidence, however, seems overwhelming that they have significant calming effects which are widely regarded as therapeutic and greatly appreciated by teachers and parents.

New developments relating to the pharmacological treatment of addiction, not only of addiction to opiates, but to other drugs as well, have been taking place. Opiate addicts, alcoholics, and other drug-dependent people constitute a most significant fraction of mentally disordered offenders.

Methadone detoxification programs, while imperfect, offer the first real possibility of a rational drug treatment of heroin addiction and, in many communities, have been claimed to contribute to the decrease in addiction related crimes. Dole and his colleagues (1968), the pioneers of methadone maintenance programs, have amply documented the beneficial effects of methadone in randomly selected criminal addicts in the New York City Correctional Institute for Men. In one study of 165 inmates, all with records of five or more jail sentences, 116 applied for methadone treatment. Twelve patients randomly selected from these applicants were started on methadone before they left prison and were then referred to the program for aftercare. None of them became readdicted to heroin and nine of the twelve had no further convictions during the 50 weeks of follow-up study. All of an untreated control group became readdicted after release from jail and 15 of 16 were convicted of new crimes during the same follow-up period.

Studies by Jaffe and his associates (1971) on acetylmethadol, a longer lasting and orally-effective, methadone-like drug, and the intense interest of pharmacological investigators in this area, argue well for the possibility of improved methadone-like treatment of addicts. It is to be hoped that improved drugs for this problem will not be subjected to the long and still continuing acceptance period that followed Dole's recognition of methadone's value.

The development of narcotic antagonists suitable for long-term treatment of addicts is still at an early stage, and the rationale for such treatment is still controversial. The intensity of work in this area, however, suggests that before long practical treatments will be available that disallow the addict to inject heroin for euphoric or other psychic effects. The "purest" antagonist drug known is a potent one named naloxone. Some of its disadvantages in the direct treatment of narcotic dependence are its low oral potency, its brief duration of action, and its cost. Another such agent, cyclazocine may circumvent some of these disadvantages, but it exerts pronounced undesirable psychic effects and may have slight narcotic effects of its own. More suitable long-lasting antagonists are being very actively sought, all the more so since top pharmaceutical industry executives have agreed to the federal government to give this area high priority in a unique cooperative venture.

One additional exploratory development with narcotic antagonists may also be alluded to at this point. It appears feasible that certain narcotic antagonists may be formulated in combination with narcotic drugs intended for oral use, not only methadone, but drugs such as codeine as well. This adulteration would have no effect on the effects of the opiates when they are administered orally, as intended, since the antagonists being considered for this purpose have negligible oral activity. Since the antagonists have marked parenteral activity, the possibility of parenteral abuse of agents such as methadone would be largely obviated.

The mentally disordered offender who most frequently appears in court, and who best epitomizes the revolving door problem, is the alcoholic. Alcoholism has stubbornly proved to be a most intractable research problem insofar as drug treatment is concerned, but even here significant advances can be discerned. Techniques enabling experimental addiction of animals to alcohol, a necessary precursor to significant laboratory research, are advancing, and much new information is being learned about the metabolism of alcohol and ways to modify it. Recent experiments (Davis and Walsh, 1970) on the formation of morphine-like substances in biological tissue exposed to alcohol, suggest that alcohol addiction and addiction to opiates may not be entirely unrelated. On the other hand, drugs such as metronidazole, which not long ago appeared to be promising in dissuading chronic alcoholics from drinking, have not proved to be effective on follow-up testing.

Perhaps the best-known drug specifically intended for therapy of alcoholics is disulfiram, an inhibitor of the enzyme, aldehyde dehydrogenase. This drug disenables the body to detoxify alcohol. Longer-lasting inhibitors or long-lasting dosage regimens may enable alcoholics to be treated in such a way that alcohol would be physically intolerable for long periods of time. There are several problems with disulfiram in addition to its sometimes serious side effects. One is that most alcoholics reject this therapy. Submission to disulfiram treatment in some clinics has been made a necessary contingency for release from confinement for the alcoholic offender. The availability of a longer-lasting drug would be of obvious value to such treatment. The moral and ethical aspects of this type of coercion have to be added to the list of contemporary legal issues in medicine.

In conclusion, psychopharmacological research has already yielded treatments of specific therapeutic value for certain classes of mentally disordered offenders. Further progress seems to be blocked by two serious problems. First, there is a dearth of people directly confronting the complex issue of developing drugs for such offenders, both in the laboratory and in prison hospitals. Secondly, social forces seem to be retarding the risk taking that is necessary for such drug development in man, even when the technical wherewithal is available. These obstacles must be surmounted. The growing numbers and varieties of mentally disordered offenders cannot be left to languish in medical and legal limbo, and no practicable alternatives to drug therapy are in sight.

REFERENCES

Clark, K. B.: Presidential Address to the Annual Meeting of the American Psychological Association, Washington, D. C., September, 1971.

Darling, H. F.: Haloperidol in 60 criminal psychotics. *Dis Nerv Syst, 32:*31, 1971.

Davis, V. E. and Walsh, M. J.: Alcohol, amines, and alkaloids: a possible biochemical basis for alcohol addiction. *Science, 167:*1005, 1970.

Dole, V. P., Nyswander, M. E., and Warner, A.: Successful treatment of 750 criminal addicts. *JAMA, 206:*2708, 1968.

Jaffe, J. H. and Senay, E. C.: Methadone and 1-methadyl acetate: use in management of narcotics addicts. *JAMA, 216:*1303, 1971.

Chapter 9

THERAPEUTIC COMMUNITY PRINCIPLES

MAXWELL JONES

Dr. Maxwell Jones and Mrs. Margaret Weeks presented a very compelling, articulate, and powerful demonstration of the processes which occur in attempting to establish a meaningful group interaction. Their presentation involved taking an unrelated group of individuals, who, working together, became an actual group which demonstrated the processes similar to those which occur in the development of a therapeutic community. However, when reduced to the printed page, the impact of this approach suffers. Therefore, the paper included here is a formal address delivered at the VI Latin American Congress of Psychiatry, 1970, San Paulo, Brazil, by Dr. Jones in which he outlines the basic principles of a therapeutic community. The contribution to clinical work which has been made by Dr. Jones as a result of his development of the therapeutic community principles has been extraordinary. His paper presents a very clear description of the major components of his approach.

EDITORS

INTRODUCTION

The concept of a therapeutic community was originally a reaction to many of the antitherapeutic practices which the author believed were prevalent in many of the psychiatric services in the United Kingdom and the United States two to three decades ago.

During World War II, great changes occurred in psychiatric practice. Immediate treatment in the front line often avoided the reinforcement of illness patterns which was likely to happen if the casualty was admitted to a base hospital. In other words, the medical expectations of a patient role were replaced by one of a functional role with rapid return to active duty.

In psychiatric hospitals during World War II, group therapy became increasingly prominent. This was partly caused by the large numbers of patients and the relative shortage of trained psychiatrists. Many other factors contributed to this change in emphasis from the one to one psychotherapy with the private psychiatrist in peacetime, to the use of the social environment to bring about change in the patient's perception of himself as a dependent and sick person. One important dimension was the increasing preoccupation with the social organization of hospitals and, in particular the role of the patient. My own experience in running a unit of 100 beds for soldiers with cardiac neurosis (called effort syndrome in the United Kingdom and neurocirculatory asthenia in the United States) forced me to recognize the importance of the patient's own peer group in promoting treatment (Jones, 1953b). By the end of the war, I was asked to run a unit of 300 beds for returned British prisoners of war from Europe and the Far East. These men had been imprisoned up to five years. They had a socially induced syndrome of "not belonging" since repatriation, were more shy than previously in the presence of women, resented the army and authority in general, feared impotency and sterility, and were insecure in relation to their families and employers (Jones and Tanner, 1947). This experience helped my colleagues and me achieve much closer involvement in the patients' lives and problems. We saw short (six weeks) hospitalization in a "transitional community" as a living-learning situation, far removed from doctor-patient interviews. We placed the men with 72 different employers in the outside world and observed their performances in these functional settings. The men lived in six cottages, each housing 50 patients. Daily meetings were scheduled to discuss the problems of living as they occurred.

This experience lasted one year and taught us much about social organization and social interaction as agents for change. Several of my colleagues then joined me in the development of a social rehabilitation unit at Belmont Hospital (later named Henderson Hospital) near London in 1947. I remained there for 12 years, working with 100 sociopaths of both sexes in an open unit. Here, we had no alternative but to ask our patients for help. We, the professional staff, made no secret of our ignorance, for we knew remarkably little about the culture and values of our largely underprivileged patient population. This was a new situation for them, for they were *needed* to explain their world to us and how working together we could help them to achieve some sort of identity and feeling of "belonging" in society. Slowly, the patients began to trust our intentions and formed a community with values and goals which were "theirs." These young men and women came from broken homes or no homes at all. They had not usually had parents whom they could use as models in their childhood development. As a result, they either actively hated society and expressed this in aggressive behavior, or they attempted to withdraw from it by seeking passive dependent roles.

My colleagues and I learned a great deal about the environmental and cultural determinents of behavior from these deprived patients. We became aware of their lack of identity, and we tried to create an environment which they could regard as theirs. Luckily, they lived in an old dilapidated building, and the damage they inflicted on windows, furniture, and woodwork was not seen in traditional administrative terms, but rather as an attack on themselves. This same reasoning applied to damage done to property outside the hospital. If their behavior resulted in a demand by the outside public that the facility should be closed (a not infrequent happening), the responsibility was not assumed by the staff alone. The patients were faced with the effects of their behavior and asked if, in fact, they wanted their facility to be closed. These were early learning experiences for both patients and staff, and slowly a greater sense of group and personal identity emerged. At the same time, the daily meetings of 100 patients and approximately 30 staff resulted in a daily analysis of behavior and its underlying meaning, as well as a critical examination of our values. This experience resulted in the emergence of a therapeutic culture which differed in many ways from the ordinary values and beliefs of outside society. Thus, honest communication came to be valued more than a polite facade, which hid one's inner feelings.

Criticism, with a view to helping the individual to know how others saw him, was seen as part of the learning situation which might help in attitude change and personality growth. Informing lost its negative quality of "telling tales out of school" and became a positive attempt to open communication with a view to learning, when the individual at risk felt unable to participate. The hypocrisy inherent in aspects of the Hippocratic oath was examined by the whole community. For example, confidentiality in the professional sense might harm rather than help the patients. Thus, a patient was seen as entitled to know, in most instances, what went on in interviews between the staff and his relatives. Indeed, we came to make a practice of never seeing a relative without the patient being present.

The admission of new patients came to be seen as a concern to staff and patients. A patient committee related to prospective patients and their relatives through an informal discussion. This experience revealed the prospective patients' expectations of "treatment" and the quality of the relationships within the family. Initially, prospective patients seemed to relate much more spontaneously with their peers than with middle class professionals. After this information-gathering process ended, the professional staff would add their skills to the evaluative process of the admission assessment group. In this way, we became aware of the expectations of prospective patients and their relatives. These expectations frequently bore little relationship to the clinical material contained in the letter from the referring doctor or agency.

In these and many other ways, my colleagues and I were beginning to develop a social organization or social system with significantly different values and beliefs than the traditional hierarchical psychiatric hospital. We were becoming "consumer conscious" and learning something about the potential for treatment inherent in the patient's own peer group. This was the route taken by some of us in arriving at the concept of a therapeutic community over the past three decades.

THERAPEUTIC COMMUNITY CONCEPTS

Every therapeutic community has its own unique social structure and culture, reflecting the personalities and training of the people within the system. Another important variable is the nature of the clinical problems being treated and the explicit goals of treatment.

The basic concept of a therapeutic community is extremely simple and is nothing more than the optimal use of the potential inherent in the patient or potential patient and his family and/or peer group, aided by the professional and paraprofessional staffs. The setting (institution, community, home, etc.) in which interaction occurs (one to one psychotherapy, family group therapy, etc.) is as important as the treatment skills available. In other words, the social organization in the natural environment of the home or in the artificial setting of a hospital ward is as important as the "treatment." In fact, the whole concept of treatment in social psychiatry is changing. As an example, a walk-in store front is becoming commonplace in the social management of drug addicts in the United States. In such settings, the addicts are not treated, that is, by a doctor looking after his patient. The addict is not put in a passive dependent role but is expected to help himself. This may take the form of the addict finding his own sponsor who may be a public health nurse, mental health worker, minister, teacher, or simply a responsible neighbor. The sponsor learns about the problems of addiction from the addict and interacts once a month with the store front personnel who can add to his knowledge and vice versa. The addict and his family accompany the sponsor on these monthly visits to the store front. The sponsor sees the addict once a week and completes an information checklist regarding the addict for the store front personnel. Such a program usually includes a methadone maintenance regime. This example illustrates a program which differs in many respects from the traditional medical treatment model.

The emphasis is on the establishment of a "healthy" social system, built around the existing (and damaged) family system. The addict is expected to help himself, but at times of stress he can turn to the store front personnel. This is not formalized treatment but part of a supportive system which includes his family, his sponsor, and the administration of methadone. The goals are cultural and ecological rather than treatment of the individual. Each addict is seen as a part of a social matrix and it is the latter which seems to be our primary concern if a more balanced society is to emerge and the lot of the individual at risk is to improve.

Social Learning

This term implies a situational, here and now, or living-learning experience. It occurs in social interaction in an informal rather than in a formalized treatment setting. The term as used here means two-way communication motivated by some inner need or stress, leading to the overt expression of feeling, and involving cognitive processes and learning. Pediatricians have for many years paid more attention to informal interaction between children and their animate or inanimate (symbolic) objects than have psychiatrists in general.

In the training of psychiatric personnel, we have tended to stress teaching or the acquisition (memorizing) of factual knowledge at the expense of learning as part of a social process. The latter is a subjective experience which results in a change of attitude and may not be accompanied by intellectual insight. Learning is aided by a heightened feeling tone or interest. This process, which is not fully understood by learning theorists, is, nevertheless, easily recognized in ourselves by introspective examination of our own attitudes. We may recognize that we have changed in certain attitudes but may have little awareness of the process of change.

Any situation of stress may be turned into a learning situation. However, the traditional hierarchical structure of a hospital, institution, or any other social unit operates against this happening. To become involved in areas of stress may be painful, time-consuming, and uncover new problems which threaten the status quo. Thus, the authority figures may find it expedient to operate in a traditional way and deal with the problem by some form of reprimand or punishment. Nothing is learned, but the situation is kept under control. Feelings of frustration are ignored.

Social learning implies a cultural attitude which encourages learning as a social process. It also implies that the authority structure is willing to become involved in situations of stress and has the experience and skill to foster a learning process.

In a therapeutic community, a specific procedure is adopted at time of crisis. For example, if two individuals are in conflict, each is asked to invite two or three of his peers to attend a confrontation. The two parties are also asked to nominate a neutral facilitator who has group dynamic skills and in whose objectivity they have confidence. This meeting must take place as soon as possible after the event. If left to the following day, all kinds of ego defenses, such as rationalization, will have emerged. While feelings are still high, these defenses are weakened and communication at a feeling level is relatively easy. These feelings aid the facilitator and the group to analyze what lies behind the behavior of both parties in the crisis situation. Interest and involvement are high and this aids the learning process.

Shared Decision Making

In a therapeutic community, a unilateral decision is seen, at best, as foolishness and, at worst, the abuse of authority; foolish because any decision affecting a group of people must involve the people concerned if they are to be identified with a positive outcome; authoritarian because no leader, however wise, can discuss a situation thoroughly with a group of colleagues without modifying his original attitude to some extent. If one accepts this thesis, then why should the leader be allowed to impose an inferior decision on his team?

Again, we are faced with the traditional hierarchical model where shared decision making may be seen as time consuming and threatening the authority of the leader.

Consensus is an abstract concept and is only relative. If, however, a mature group of professionals are asked to arrive at consensus, then everyone will recognize the need for compromise if a decision is to be made. This very process is a learning experience. In favorable circumstances, individual attitudes will change in the direction of a common goal with which everyone is identified. If, however, some individuals believe that their personal integrity or beliefs prevent such a compromise, then consensus becomes impossible for the time being at least. The issue may be left on the table and discussed again at some future date or it may be forgotten. The leader may insist on *his* solution being accepted and ignore the lack of consensus. Pressure from above or sheer expediency may force him to make a unilateral decision. In such a case, the outcome will usually be less successful as judged by his colleagues. In the case of failure, he stands alone.

Leadership

In a therapeutic community, multiple leadership in a multidisciplinary organization replaces the usual hierarchical structure affecting each of the professional disciplines. In the latter, status is important and the spectrum from doctor to patient is rigidly enforced. In a therapeutic community, roles tend to be blurred. Nurses involved in community work may play roles indistinguishable from social workers or psychiatrists. Even in the hospital setting, ward teams may have social workers, psychologists, physicians, or nurses as team leaders. This happens at Fort Logan Mental Health Center, Denver, Colorado. Unfortunately, the old status differentiation is still manifest in the various pay scales.

There are many advantages if the authority structure tends to be horizontal rather than vertical. In the earlier part of this paper, I stressed the growing awareness of the importance of the patient's own peer group and his need to assume responsibility for his own problems. This led to consideration of his family and other systems and the establishment, when possible, of a more healthy social system. In this context, we are paying more attention than is usual in psychiatric practice to the patient's own potential for leadership. Some credit is due, I think, to the therapeutic community approach which over the past two or three decades has questioned the whole authority structure of hospitals and demonstrated the advantages of a democratic egalitarian model. However, professional staff still generally filled the leadership roles, while the patients and the less qualified professionals and para-professionals had to be content with very limited leadership roles.

The whole question of leadership in social psychiatry is in a state of flux. In a community mental health program, leadership from the citizens has to be blended with professional leadership. However, for the first time in the history of modern psychiatry, professional leadership is seen as subservient to the needs and wishes of the community, as expressed by its leaders. Citizens are confused and alarmed by this new responsibility which is expected of them. They cannot, as yet, do without professional guidance, and integration of effort must, in the final analysis, depend upon shared common concern and determination to improve the circumstances in which the social casualties live. This is the therapeutic community of the future, where the social systems which constitute society have an awareness of their own potentiality to bring about change, and the professional is merely a facilitator of this change.

REFERENCES

Jones, Maxwell: *Beyond the Therapeutic Community.* New Haven, Yale, 1968a.

Jones, Maxwell: *The Therapeutic Community.* New York, Basic Books, 1953b.

Jones, Maxwell and Polak, Paul: Crisis and confrontation. *Br J Psychiatr, 114*:169, 1968.

Jones, Maxwell and Tanner, James: Clinical characteristics, treatment and rehabilitation of repatreated prisoners of war with neurosis. *J Neurol Neurosurg Psychiatry, 11*:53, 1948.

Chapter 10

BEHAVIOR MODIFICATION WITH THE DELINQUENT OFFENDER

JOHN BURCHARD

Very little published material has been concerned with the application of specific treatment modalities to the mentally disordered offender population. In recent years, behavior modification techniques have become more widely used with clinical populations. In his paper, Dr. John Burchard discusses some of the specific attempts to apply learning principles in a treatment setting. Following his presentation of examples, Dr. Burchard raises two additional pertinent issues. Specifically, he addresses himself to the problems of undesirable side effects of learning approaches and the need to focus on the problems of generalization of such techniques.

EDITORS

In recent years, there has been a remarkable increase in the application of learning principles to the broad areas of education, treatment, and rehabilitation (Bandura, 1969, Bradfield, 1970, Franks, 1969, and Ulrich, *et al.* 1966). This has been particularly true in the areas of crime and delinquency, where programs variously labeled behavior modification, behavior therapy, operant conditioning, and reinforcement therapy have been developed in prisons, training schools, institutions, halfway houses, and community-based prevention programs.

Although behavior modification programs differ markedly in terms of the specific procedures they utilize, each one is usually based on the general assumption that there is a functional relationship between antisocial behavior and the environment in which it occurs. Granted this assumption, then it becomes clear that one way to change delinquent behavior is to change the environment. This, then, is probably the basic difference between the behavior modification approach and some of the more traditional psychological and psychiatric methods of rehabilitating criminals and delinquents. Instead of trying to change the per-

111

son through some type or periodic psychotherapeutic or verbal mediation, the focus is on changing the environment so that appropriate behaviors are strengthened or weakened. In general, the environment is arranged so that adaptive behavior is strengthened through rewarding consequences, and maladaptive or antisocial behavior is weakened through nonrewarding and/or punishing consequences.

There seems to be little question that the behavior modification approach has been productive and that much of the present enthusiasm is warranted. Let me briefly describe four different programs which give rise to such optimism, two which relate to prevention and two which relate to rehabilitation.

One of the preventive programs was developed by Tharp and Wetzel (1969) in Arizona while the second one is presently being conducted by Bailey and his colleagues (1970) as well as others (Phillips, 1968) at the University of Kansas. In both instances, the population consisted of adolescent boys who displayed a high frequency of antisocial behavior, but they had not been adjudicated as delinquents. Also, in both programs, the basic procedure was to arrange the environment so that rewards were contingent upon small, successive approximations of adaptive behavior in a variety of situations. The main difference was that the Arizona project was conducted in the natural environment with boys residing at home, while the Kansas project was conducted within a home style, residential setting (Achievement Place). While it is still too early to properly assess the effects of either program, preliminary studies have been quite impressive. Through the systematic manipulation of reinforcement contingencies, high frequencies of intolerable, disruptive behavior have been replaced by behavior which is much more adaptive and related to community survival.

Both of the rehabilitation programs I will briefly describe took place within correctional facilities. One was developed by Cohen and his associates (Cohen, J. L., 1968 and Cohen, H. L., 1968) at the National Training School when it was located in Washington, D.C. The other program was developed (Clements and McKee, 1968) at Draper Prison in Alabama. In both programs the environment was arranged so that aversive consequences were minimized and inmates did not have to do anything to obtain the basic necessities of penal life. However, for those who wanted to improve their life style, points or marks could be earned through small units of academic achievement and cashed in for more interesting food, special privileges, opportunities to spend time in a recreation lounge, and occasional trips away from the institution. As a result of these systems, the attitudes of the inmates greatly improved and, on a voluntary basis, they began to spend long hours on their schoolwork and related behavior problems were greatly decreased.

As mentioned above, the results of these programs are impressive and the enthusiasm of their proponents seems warranted. However, the entire picture regarding the future of behavior modification does not consist of unqualified optimism. It seems clear that the behavior modification approach will not be the final phase in the rehabilitation of delinquents and criminals, at least not at the state in which behavior modification is in today. There is considerable historical evidence that new treatment approaches, if they are to survive at all, are initially met with overwhelming attention and enthusiasm, are hailed as the solution to all problems, and are included in the treatment armament of most respectable institutions and agencies. However, once the initial dust has settled, the really significant issues begin to arise. Due to the objective, empirical nature of many behavior modification programs, the question of whether or not behavior can really be modified has already received an affirmative answer, at least with respect to many different, overt behaviors. There are other issues, however, which currently plague the development and possibly even the survival of the behavior modification approach.

Basically, the issues I am referring to relate to what constitutes behavior modification, the manner in which it should be applied with criminals and delinquents, and the need to go beyond the repeated demonstration of the law of effect (Thorndike, 1932) and focus on the more important problem of generalization or the transition from the artificial or controlled environment to the natural environment. Without further emphasis and investigation on these issues, it is likely that behavior modification will go the way of many fads.

Much of what I have to say with respect to these issues stems from my own personal experience over the past five years developing a behavior modification program for delinquent retardates at Murdoch Center, in North Carolina (Burchard, 1967). Since we did not anticipate these issues, I have referred to them as unforeseen contingencies. However, on the basis of what I have seen, heard, and read about other behavior modification programs, I am convinced that there are three basic issues that relate to the general status of behavior modification. I will try to describe each one as concisely as possible.

First, there appears to be considerable confusion with respect to what constitutes behavior modification (Birnbrauer *et al.,* 1970). While it is generally agreed that the techniques are derived from or are consistent with the principles of learning, that is, shaping, prompting, fading, reinforcement, extinction, punishment, etc., there is considerable variation in the manner in which these techniques are applied. For example, in many situations, behavior modification merely connotes the administration of certain procedures. Predetermined behaviors are rewarded, ignored, or punished through contingency management. However, there is no systematic data collection of analysis to provide empirical verification of the effects of these procedures. Procedures are selected and maintained on *a priori* basis (they were shown to be effective in someone else's program) or on the basis of good common sense (television is reinforcing for most kids). Unfortunately, good common sense or knowing what works with others is not good enough, especially in working with delinquents and criminals. It would seem that if the solution were that simple, then the problems would have been solved a long time ago.

One of the major assets of the behavior modification approach is that it is amenable to continuous, empirical verification. Procedures can be selected, maintained, and modified on the basis of their effects on behavior and not on the basis of common sense, subjective impression, or guesswork. This emphasis on the dynamic aspect of behavior modification, the interaction between procedure and effect, has resulted in the process being relabeled applied behavior analysis (Baer *et al.*, 1968). My main point, then, is that systematic empirical analysis of the effects of specific behavior modification procedures should be an integral part of every behavior modification program. Without carefully defining and monitoring the behaviors to be modified, the value of a behavior modification is extremely limited.

The second issue pertains to the manner in which behavior modification programs should be applied, especially with delinquents and criminals. There is little question regarding the power of contingency management. If the consequences are of sufficient magnitude, whether positive or negative, it is relatively easy to produce at least a temporary change in behavior. But are there any negative side effects associated with that change in behavior? It is a question which warrants further consideration.

Much has been written regarding the possible negative side effects of aversive control. While punishment or the threat of punishment frequently results in an immediate change in behavior, it weakens the relationship (or, in behavioral terms, the reinforcement contingency) between the person who administers and the person who receives the punishment. Also, although punishment may produce a persistent effect in the presence of the punishing agent, there is the question of the effect in the absence of the punishing agent. At least in some situations, punished behavior occurs more frequently in the absence of the punishing agent.

Negative side effects may not occur only in the context of punishment. There is some evidence that for some individuals the process of managing reinforcement contingencies, even where the contingencies are primarily positive, produces undesirable side effects. The negative side effect is that after the contingency is removed, the behavior which was previously required to get a particular consequence occurs less frequently than it did before the contingency was applied. For example, an adolescent is told that in order to be able to watch television at night, he must clean his room. Because television is a powerful reinforcer for this particular individual, he cleans his room while the contingency is in effect. However, after the contingency is removed, he cleans his room less often than he did before the contingency was applied. Is this because he wants the contingency to be reinstated? Or is it because he does not think that you believe that it is important that he cleans his room anymore? Or is it because of something else? The reaction is similar to what some social psychologists refer to as reactance, a motivational opposition to a decrease in freedom (Brehm, 1966). Certainly, one's freedom is limited in a contingency management program, especially one in which the consequences one previously enjoyed on a noncontingent basis are all of a sudden made contingent upon some difficult or undesirable behavior.

The point I am trying to make is that in administering a behavior modification program, the guiding principle should not be to utilize the procedure which produces the greatest and most immediate change in behavior. Depending upon the procedure and how it is administered, it is possible that there will be negative side effects which will be incompatible with long-range goals. This is particularly true with punishment and may even be true in programs in which the contingency management involves gross or unsubtle limits of choice or freedom. On numerous occasions, I have been asked why the old training school-reformatory point systems proved to be so ineffective when they appeared to involve contingency management. It appears to me that the contingency management used in those programs were based almost entirely upon aversive control. Either one behaved or he lost something desirable. Possibly, it is reinforcing not to engage in such behavior in the absence of such control, call it reactance or whatever.

The final issue pertains to the problem of generalization. As mentioned above, there is little question regarding the power of behavior modification techniques. In most instances, it has been found that a behavior can be modified in a desirable direction if the consequences, especially the immediate consequences, can be manipulated or controlled. However, in the process of controlling a consequence, an artificial contingency is introduced. While the artificial contingency may produce successful behavior modification, there is still the question of how to bring the modified behavior under the control of natural contingencies. To illustrate the problem, it may be possible to get a delinquent youth to display good manners by paying him tokens for successive approximations of appropriate behavior at mealtime. Depending upon the severity of the problem, establishing good table manners could be an impressive and worthy achievement even though accomplished through artificial contingencies. However, if the rehabilitation or habilitation is to be complete, it is necessary to eventually bring the good table manners under the control of natural contingencies. There are few places in society where a person will get paid for displaying good manners.

Due to the behaviorists' zeal for empirical verification, or at least some behaviorists, the magnitude of the problem is demonstrated repeatedly. That is, in order to demonstrate that a particular technique has produced a significant change in behavior, the behavior modifier will frequently switch from the treatment conditions (the artificial contingency) to a no treatment condition (which frequently represents the natural contingency). This is the typical ABA experimental design. What the behavior modifier typically finds is that once the treatment conditions (the artificial contingencies) are removed, the behavior quickly reverts back to its pretreatment level or frequency. To use an example with table manners, once good table manners were established, the tokens might be removed (or administered noncontingently) to see if it was the contingent administration of tokens that produced the good table manners. Under such conditions, one is likely to find that the level or frequency of good table manners will decline.

While it is necessary to perform manipulations, such as those involved in the ABA design, it is important not to stop with the demonstration of a casual relationship between a behavior and a particular consequence. The fact that the behavior deteriorates when the contingency is changed or removed points out the problem of generalization. It is time for those involved in behavior modification programs to move beyond the repeated demonstration of the law of effect and to focus more on building increased resistance to those effects. Although there have been some efforts in this direction, more research is needed.

To summarize, I began by pointing out the increasing appeal of the use of behavior modification with criminals and delinquents and gave several examples of sound programs in the area of prevention and rehabilitation. At the same time, I have tried to point out that, in my opinion, the behavior modification approach has not solved all of the problems and that, in fact, there are several issues which presently plague its effectiveness. In general, these issues relate to the need to establish behavior modification programs on an empirical or analytic basis, the need to focus on possible side effects which are incompatible with long-range goals, and finally, the need to go beyond a demonstration of the power of behavior modification techniques and focus on problems of generalization.

REFERENCES

Baer, D. M., Wolf, M. M. and Risley, T. R.: Some current dimensions of applied behavior analysis. *J Appl Behav Anal 1*:91, 1968.

Bailey, J. S., Wolf, M. M. and Phillips, E. L.: Home-based reinforcement and the modification of pre-delinquents' classroom behavior. *J Appl Behav Anal, 3*:223, 1970.

Bandura, Albert: *Principles of Behavior Modification.* New York, Holt, Rinehart and Winston, 1969.

Birnbrauer, J. S., Burchard, J. D. and Burchard, Sara N.: Wanted: behavior analysts. In Bradfield, R. H. (Ed.): *Behavior Modification: the Human Effort.* San Rafael, Dimensions, 1970.

Bradfield, Robert H. (Ed.): *Behavior Modification: The Human Effort.* San Rafael, Dimensions, 1970.

Brehm, J. W.: *A Theory of Psychological Reactance.* New York, Academic, 1966.

Burchard, J. D.: Systematic socialization: a programmed environment for the habilitation of antisocial retardates. *Psychol Rec, 11*:461, 1967.

Clements, C. B. and McKee, J. M.: Programmed instruction for institutionalized offenders: contingency management and performance contracts. *Psychol Rep, 22*:957, 1968.

Cohen, J. L.: Educational therapy: the design of learning environments. In Shlien, J. M. (Ed.): *Research in Psychotherapy.* Washington, American Psychological Association, 1968.

Cohen, H. L., Filipaczak, J., Bis, J., Cohen, J., Goldiamond, I. and Larkin, P.: *Case II—Model: A Contingency-Oriented 24-Hour Learning Environment in a Juvenile Correctional Institution.* Silver Spring, Educational Facility Press, 1968.

Franks, Cyril M. (Ed.): *Behavior Therapy: Appraisal and Status.* New York, McGraw-Hill, 1969.

Phillips, E. L.: Achievement place: token reinforcement procedures in a home-style rehabilitation setting for "pre-delinquent" boys. *J Appl Behav Anal, 1:*213, 1968.

Tharp, R. G. and Wetzel, R. J.: *Behavior Modification in the Natural Environment.* New York, Academic Press, 1969.

Thorndike, E. L.: Reward and punishment in animal learning. *Comp Psychol Mono,* No. 39, 1932.

Ulrich, Roger, Stachnik, Thomas and Mabry, John (Eds.): *Control of Human Behavior.* Glenview, Scott, Foresman, 1966, Vols. I and II.

Chapter 11

THE TALKING CRIMINAL: A BIOLOGICAL AND POLITICAL PHENOMENON

Guy Mersereau

Dr. Guy Mersereau has been able to gain a perspective on the problems of the mentally disordered offender from his work at a county forensic psychiatry service. He is concerned about communication between the criminal justice and mental health systems and he fears that there has been a serious blockage between the two. He presents some suggestions as to how we can begin to repair the damage and, at the same time, he raises the issues as to whether it is too late.

Editors

The iron gate was locked behind me for the last time. The summer sun is brilliant in the courtyard. The dark human figure with his lethal *carabine* [sic] walks as always on the wall. The wall stands, grey as always, all around me. Grey but no longer cold. Why not cold? It always had been, the dark cruel oppressor, the barrier to any joy. Now suddenly my wall is warm! It holds me still but soon will let me go. Now still it stretches out before me and I walk in its embrace.

My prison has become my home! No, more my mother's arms, and breast.

The passage quoted here was obviously written by someone leaving prison and describing a sudden attack of nostalgia. He is suddenly aware of how much prison had come to mean to him, how infantile and dependent upon it he had become. In short, how much a prisoner. We are very familiar with this institutionalization of the inmate in chronic hospitals. We are gaining, too, a fair appreciation of this process in prison. Knowing this, and knowing how debilitating it can be, we have become much more sparing and selective in our use of the hospital. Psychiatry, particularly in the past decade, has shifted its main base of operation from the hospital to the community. It was part of this movement to the community that led to the establishment of our Forensic Psychiatry Service in Erie County, New York, about two years ago.

The function of this service is to provide mental health consultation to the criminal justice system in Erie County. Thus, in addition to the courts, it serves the jail, penitentiary, probation, parole, and police departments. Prior to its inception, such referrals, primarily from the courts, were made mainly to the department of psychiatry at the county hospital, which had 13 beds set aside for this purpose. The new service is based downtown in its main office, which is located next door to the Buffalo City Court on the one side and the Erie County Jail on the other. Across the street are the County, Family, and Supreme Courts, as well as the offices of the Department of Probation and the District Attorney. We keep the 13 beds at the county hospital, but these are empty most of the time. Inpatient treatment is carried on by the service in the jail and penitentiary infirmaries. Numbers of referrals continue to rise, but more come now from the jail than from all the courts combined. The focus of the service has gradually shifted from the individual client to the system in which he is involved. There is a tendency for clinicians and other professionals to deny such supra-individual systems and we, too, have fallen into this in spite of our mandate to serve those systems. We were brought up rather sharply on this when charges were pressed for several rapes on the under 21 galleries at the jail. The jailer asked for help and we then started meeting with groups of inmates from the cellblocks involved. These meetings became institutionalized on a weekly basis and are still continuing. We had already been conducting therapy groups of comparable size and very soon the two types of groups became virtually indistinguishable. In either case, the starting point was institutional problems as these were most immediately relevant and meaningful to the inmates. The main problems discussed related closely to leaving the institution. Hence, there was a preoccupation with the boundary of the system in terms of separation from it. This was the concern with which this paper began. The insights gained at this time can be applied by the individual in building a better life for himself outside, but very often not, it seems, without further help. Therefore, a follow-through after release by those who knew him inside is of utmost importance. Unfortunately, this usually is not done. We have made some beginnings in tackling this problem by extending our service to a self-help group of ex-inmates.

It can be seen, then, that we have found and engaged an inmate system and an ex-inmate system as well as the more institutionalized counter-criminal system which we are mandated to serve. The dynamic interaction between a criminal and counter-criminal system was seen in the therapeutic community at the Diagnostic and Treatment Center of Clinton Prison, Dannemora, New York, between guards and inmates (Cormier and Williams, 1970). It is a defensive posture of paranoid positions facing each other characteristic of institutions which are built as closed systems. The strain is produced by the inherent openness of being alive and the more reciprocal responsive relationships required by this. In the therapeutic community, we opened the system to a considerable degree by leveling the staff hierarchy, democratizing control, and blurring professional roles (Jones, 1968). Here, however, there was minimal follow-through at best after release, and the many gains which were seen inside appeared to be lost afterwards.

Another failure has been our lack of understanding of the degree to which the staff of the institution has become institutionalized. Within any institution, territorial kingdoms of all sizes and kinds are formed, with everyone a ruler over some thing which he jealously defends against encroachment. At Clinton Prison, the visitor is struck by the "courts" which they call their little patches of land on which they grow things, build little huts, and keep their belongings. The system is used for control, but still fights occur over possessions and boundaries. Similar territorial systems are described in mental hospitals, especially on the more chronic wards, and, of course, in other biosystems. What we see within the system, we see also between systems, particularly in those Ping-Pong games in which an individual is bounced back and forth between one system and another (Mersereau, 1971). Situated as we are in the interface between criminal justice and mental health systems, we are constantly dealing with this kind of problem. Problems like alcoholism, borderline mental states, severe character disorders, and malingering, which are most susceptible to different definitions and labels, as well as being most troublesome and unlovely, are frequently caught in this process. What we see is differential labeling, the guard calling him sick, and the doctor calling him criminal. These are the verbal messages, but behind them are rather different messages which are transmitted nonverbally in the actual transfer of the person in question. These messages are saying bilaterally, "We don't want him; you take him."

Thus, analyzing the communication at this level, one finds no semantic difference between the messages sent from either side. They differ only in direction. This problem is thus susceptible to the same analysis that has been applied to other conflict situations, such as between husband and wife as well as "The Watcher and the Watched," where the escalation of the interaction is related to differential punctuation of the series of events (Watzlawick *et al.*, 1967). Different systems, such as medical and legal ones, turn out on this scrutiny to be not so different. Both are competing to do as little new work as possible and conservatively resist any change. The need to keep one's own place in his own way is as strong as is the threat to change that place and that way. It also grows with time and lack of change. This, then, is institutionalization. It was felt by that person who was described at the beginning as he left the institution. That person was not an inmate. He was one of the staff.

What can we do about it? At the level of the individual client, we treat it mainly with talking. Our skill in this depends more upon our listening than talking ourselves. By the time problems come to us, however, the communication has become so distorted that it takes a while to figure it out. We must establish common language before we can begin to understand each other. Often, words of any kind have become so suspect that the main communication must, at the beginning, be through nonverbal acts. This is often the case with the criminal, whose style is usually more action oriented. This is so true that the concept of the talking criminal is almost a contradiction in terms. It strikes a jarring note, both to those of us who know criminals and to those who know only the popular stereotype. We all know that a good criminal doesn't talk. To talk is to break one of the most heavily sanctioned rules of the criminal code. One immediately suspects an informer or rat. Talk, where used, is not to inform, but rather to deceive, as in a con job, so that if a criminal does talk, one is inclined to suspect that he is lying. Well, we do encounter quite a few prevaricators in our work. Often, when we do, the con game has by then ceased to be fun and the criminal is looking for a better way. Before we look ahead to find that better way, we look behind to find out why he is where he is. When we do that, we find that the prevaricator has been lied to and has come to distrust words whose main value he sees as aggressive tools or weapons. First, we must restore some trust and we must do it nonverbally, demonstrating our good will through consistently helpful acts. It's still difficult to get very far in jail or prison with this because trust requires some freedom. Within the more open setting of a therapeutic community, we know that a lot can be done, but we have found with therapy groups of parolees that we can achieve this trust more readily outside. Then we can really talk. Our service has reached this stage also with the larger systems we serve. We are demonstrating good faith and helpfulness and just beginning to talk.

We had come to see ourselves in this way, as physicians to the larger systems, opening closed systems, and heading, hopefully, towards community corrections when the Attica Prison riot occurred. We could say we saw it coming, and in a sense we did, but in another equally valid sense, we were caught napping. We had watched the growing political awareness, especially of Black inmates, and a correspondingly increasing group cohesiveness and solidarity. There was an increasing trend to see oneself as a victim of an oppressive and exploitative society. Such complaints of victimization, whatever their validity, we would handle with the individual in therapy as a projection, cop out, or denial of his own responsibility. This approach can still be quite effective. Increasingly, however, we were seeing another path taken, the path of Malcolm X where, through a religious kind of conversion, the old antisocial ways were given up in favor of working for one's brothers. This had a powerful and dramatic effect in the lives of these individuals, much more than we were able to achieve through our most intensive therapeutic efforts. We had known a few prisoners who were in for mainly political reasons. They were quite strikingly different from the other criminals we knew in their passionate concern for society. The others we could describe as dyssocial, antisocial, or asocial with remarkably little concern for others. Now, however, many of these apparently common criminals are calling themselves political prisoners; they are no longer content with their self ascribed role of victim. We must see the validity of this and are forced now to consider the political dimension of any crime.

How can we put all this together? Biologically, we know that all living systems operate by the same principles, whether they are intracellular microsystems or the largest ecosystems. They are first of all self regulating and, therefore, open systems (von Bertalanffy, 1966). Separate subsystems process high (motive) energy and low (signal) energy. There is an aging process during which they become less responsive or flexible and, therefore, relatively more closed until death finally supervenes. This closure and hardening of the system is marked by the failure of (especially) the signal subsystems. This we can see occurring with communicational distortions progressing to complete blockage. Some of these distortions have been described above as differential labeling, double messages, and differential punctuation. We have learned to deal with them, reverse their deteriorating course, and restore better function in both verbal and nonverbal modalities. The ease with which we can do this depends on how far the disease has progressed. When objective signs supervene and predominate over subjective symptoms, it is often too late. The question now is how closed and how near death is the criminal justice system? It seems that it may be well past healing by merely administrative reform. Is it also past political reform? Can we still maximize and develop those parts, like the tacit part of the guard-inmate interaction, where we see openness? And how, more politically, can we work reform from outside the system? Otherwise, is a more violent revolution inevitable? If we have a real democracy it shouldn't be, but then how democratic are our institutions?

Finally, to do all this, where will we get the money? It is proposed that those who are concerned about these questions form a political lobby and press actively for the formation of those open institutions which we agree are needed. The need is urgent. We must act now for it will soon be too late.

REFERENCES

Cormier, B. and Williams, P.: The watcher and the watched. *Can Psychiatr Assoc J, 16:*1, 1970.

Jones, Maxwell: *Social Psychiatry in Practice.* Baltimore, Penguin, 1968.

Mersereau, G.: The Criminal in General Systems: A Mental Health Consultation Service to the Criminal Justice System in One County. Paper delivered at American Society of Criminology, San Juan, Puerto Rico. November, 1971.

Watzlawick, Paul, Beavin, Janet H. and Jackson, Don D.: *The Pragmatics of Human Communication.* New York, Norton, 1967.

von Bertalanffy, L.: General systems theory and psychiatry. In Arieti, S. (Ed.): *American Handbook of Psychiatry.* New York, Basic Books, 1966, Vol. III, pp. 705-717.

INDEX

A

Abrahamsen, D., 4
Acetylmethadol, 99
Adam & Eve, 86
Addiction, 98
Addicts, 106-107
Administrative Office of U. S. Supreme
    Court, 92
Adolescent boys, 112
Aging process, 125
Aggression
    psychopathy, 8
    neurosis, 8
Alcatraz, 86
Alcoholics, 98
Alcoholism, 100
Aldehyde, 100
Allstrom, D., 8
American colonies, 86
American corrections, 83
American Federal Penitentiary, 86
American Psychiatric Association, 36
American Psychological Association, 95
American Revolution, 85
Amitriptyline, 97
Amsterdam, 86
Amphetamine, 97, 98
Anatomical characteristics, 95
Animate or inanimate objects, 107
Antianxiety drugs, 97
Antidepressants, 97
Antipsychotic medication, 96
Applied behavioral analysis, 115
Arizona Project, 112
Attica Prison, 83, 124
Auburn Prison, 85

B

Baer, D. M., 115
Bailey, J. S., 112

Bandura, Albert, 111
Barr, Norman, 84
Bavarian Code, 87
Bazelon, David, 55, 68
Beavin, Janet, 123
Behavior Modification
    basic differences, 111-112
    general assumptions, 111-112
    issues described, 114-117
    issues identified, 113-114
    major asset, 114-115
    preventive programs, 112
    rehabilitation programs, 112-113
    summary, 118
Bellevue Hospital, 8
Belmont Hospital, 75, 103
Benzodiazepines, 97-98
Binger, C., 22
Birnbrauer, J. S., 114
Bis, J., 112
Bluestone, H., 5
Boorstin, D. J., 22
Bradfield, Robert H., 111
Brehm, J. W., 116
Bridewell Prison, 87, 88
Brodsky, Stanley, 5
Bromberg, W., 5
Bulgaria, 9
Burchard, J. D., 114
Burchard, Sara N., 114
Bureau of Prisons, 92
Burger, Warren, 91
Butyrophenones, 96

C

Calhoun, Karen, 11
California Commission Report, 83-84
Campus prisons, 88-90
Canada, 11-12
Cardiac neurosis, 103
Carolina Colonies, 85

127

Casper, Elizabeth, 4
Cerebral arteriosclerosis, 9
Charles V, 87
Chemicals, endogenous, 94
Cherry Hill Prison, 85
Chicago, 10
Chlordiazepoxide, 97
Chlorpromazine, 96
Chronic alcoholism, 100
Claghorn, James L., 11
Clark, Kenneth, 95
Cleckley, Hervey, 35
Clements, C. B., 112
Clinton Prison, 122
Codeine, 100
Cohen, H. L., 112
Cohen, J. L., 112
College students
  mental health, 7
Commonwealth v. Harrison, 41
Community prisons, 90-91
Community treatment centers, 91
Competency to stand trial
  behavioral indices, 41
  commitment, 46
  failure to consider, 65
  frequency, 5, 37
  historical development, 39
  judicial definition, 41
  lack of treatment, 48-49
  legal maneuver, 43-46
  mental illness, 38-39
  objective criteria, 49
  requirements for, 58
  return to trial, 46-47
  statutory definition, 39-41
Confrontation, 80-81
Congregate system, 85-86
Consumer conscience, 105
Cook, Richard A., 5
Cormier, B., 122
Corrections
  public support, 82-84
Cottage system, 86
Criminals, mentally ill, 4
Criminally insane, 4
Criminal sexual psychopath, 31

Crofton, 87
Cyclazocine, 99

D

Darling, H. F., 96
Davis, V. E., 100
Dehydrogenase, 100
Delinquent retardates, 114
Democratic society, 82
Dennissenko, S. G., 9
de Reuck, A. V. S., 9
Diagnosis, 8
Diagnostic and treatment center, 122
Diazepam, 97
Diminished Responsibility, 30
Disulfiram, 100-101
Dole, V. P., 98-99
Doxepin, 97
Draper Prison, 112
Drug addiction, 6-7
Dunham, H. W., 10
Durham Rule, 28, 29, 30, 42, 57
Dusley v. U. S., 41

E

Effort Syndrome, 103
Ego defenses, 108
Elmira Reformatory, 85
Endogenous depression, 97
Enzyme, 100
Epilepsy
  crime, 8
  murder, 8
Erickson, Eric, 79
Erie County Jail, 121
Executive branch, 92-93

F

Father Cook, 87
Federal Bureau of Prisons, 84, 91, 92
Filipaczak, J., 112
Fink, Ludwig, 15

Forensic psychiatry, 67, 121
Fort Logan Mental Health Center, 109
Franks, Cyril M., 111
Freud, Sigmund, 70
Fry, Elizabeth, 87-88

G

Gaol Act, 87
Gibbens, T. C. N., 10
Glasser, William, 90
Goldiamond, I., 112
Great Britain, 85

H

Haloperidol, 96
Hamburger, Ernest, 13
Hartogs, Renatus, 55, 56, 57
Hayek, F. A., 21
Henderson Hospital, 75, 76, 103
Heroin addiction, 98
Hippies, 74
Hippocratic Oath, 105
Hospice of St. Michel, 88
House of Refuge, 86
Howard, John, 87
Humane rehabilitation, 86-87
Hyperkinetic children, 98

I

Imipramine, 97
Illinois Revised Statutes, 39
Illinois Security Hospital, 10
Indeterminate sentencing, 87-88
Indiana, 86
Industrial Revolution, 85
Inmate labor, 88
Insanity
    bizarre crimes, 61
    failure to plead, 63-64
    frequency, 62
    time of execution, 43
    time of offense, 42

time of trial, 39
Institutionalization, 122-123
Intracellular microsystems, 125
Irresistible Impulse Test, 28, 29, 30

J

Jackson, Don D., 123
Jaffe, J. H., 99
Jones, Maxwell, 75, 77, 79, 80, 81, 103, 122
Judicial administration, 91-93
Justice
    contracts, 19
    problems in definition, 18-20
Justinian Code, 86

K

Kanno, C. K., 5, 37
Kansas, 12
Kansas Project, 112
Kent State University, 83
Kloek, J., 7

L

Lanzkron, J., 6
Larkin, P., 112
Law
    dispositional process, 51-53
    logic, 52
    mental health, 53-54, 56, 68-70
    need for psychiatrists, 59-60
Leadership, 109
Lennon, W. G., 8
Lipsitt, P. D., 49
Lobenthal, Joseph, 4, 55
Lombroso, 87
Lorton Reformatory, 86
Lyons, John A., 7

M

MacCurdy, Frederick, 7
Maconachie, 87-88

Maison de Force, 88
Malcolm X, 125
Mania, 96
Manson, Charles, 61
Marby, John, 111
Maryland, 13
Massachusetts, 87
Matson, F., 21
Matteawan State Hospital, 9
Maximum security, 85-86
McGarry, Louis, 47
McGee, Richard, 7
McKee, J. M., 112
McKerracher, D. W., 11
McKnight, C. K., 11
Medical Center for Federal Prisoners, 84
Mentally disordered children, 98
Mentally disordered offender, 95-98,
   100-101
   ages, 1
   defined, 4
   description, 6
   diagnosis, 7, 14
   frequency, 5, 12-13
   legal definitions, 33
   outcome, 13
   therapy, 14
   types, 5-6
Menninger, Karl, 21, 23, 24, 25, 42, 55,
   65
Mental illness
   brain injury, 8-9
   culture, 8
   emergency hospitalization, 32-33
   race, 8
   responsibility, 4
   role expectation, 3
   self-mutilation, 7
   temporary confinement, 32
Mersereau, G., 122
Messinger, E., 6-7
Metabolites, 94
Methadone, 100
   detoxification programs, 98-99
Metronidazole, 100
Mill, John S., 19
Minority populations, 83

M'Naghten Rule, 28, 29, 30, 42, 44, 48,
   57, 70
Model Penal Code, 28, 30, 42, 43, 57
Morality and medicine, 22
Morphine, 100
Murder, 6, 8
Murdock Center, 114

N

Naloxone, 99
Narcotic antagonists, 99-100
National Training School, 112
Neurocirculatory asthenia, 103
Neuromodulators, 94
Neurotransmitters, 94
New York City Correctional Institute
   for Men, 99
New York City prison system, 97
Not guilty by reason of insanity, 6, 37
Nyswander, M. E., 98-99

O

Opiate addicts, 98
Opiates, 100

P

Paranoid hostility and aggressiveness,
   96
Parkhurst, 86
Penitentiary House, 85
Phenothiazines, 96
Phillips, E. L., 112
Plato, 85
Polak, Paul, 80
Podolsky, E., 7
Police
   characteristics, 33
   needs, 34
Pond, D. A., 8
Porter, Ruth, 9
President's Task Force on Corrections,
   90

Prisons
    program development, 86-88
    public attitude, 82-84
    selective prisons, 85-86
    social system, 75-81
    woman, 86
Prisoners
    mental illness, 7, 12, 13
Probation, 92
Psychopharmacology, 101

R

Rappeport, Jonas R., 13
Rauhus Haus, 85
Reactive depression, 97
Reagan, Ronald, 83
Reality Therapy, 90
Reformatory, 85
Rehabilitation, 76
Reich, Charles, 74-75
Risley, T. R., 115
Robey, Ames, 39, 41, 42
Rollin, Henry, 9
Ruby, Jack, 61
Rush, Benjamin, 21, 22, 23, 87

S

Sadoff, Robert L., 4
Salten, Joseph, 12
San Quentin, 83
Scheff, Thomas, 3
Scheidemandel, Patricia L., 5, 37
Schipkowensky, N., 9
Schizophrenia, 7, 8
Security, 85-86
Senay, E. C., 99
Sex offenders
    age, 8
    hospital admissions, 5
    mental illness, 7
    statutory definition, 30-32
Silverman, Daniel, 10
Sirhan, Sirhan, 61
Social learning, 80, 103, 107-108

Social systems
    culture, 74
    definition, 73
    types, 73-76
Sociopath, 7, 34-36
Spanish Inquisition, 85
Stachnik, Thomas, 111
Szasz, Thomas 4, 23, 26, 42, 55, 56

T

Tanner, James, 103
Tattoos, 11
Texas, 11
Tharp, R. G., 112
Therapeutic Community, 122, 124
    basic concepts, 106-110
    leadership, 109-110
    shared decision making, 108-109
    social learning, 107-108
    variables, 105-106
Therapeutic culture, 75
Therapeutic state, 23
Thiothixene, 96
Thioxanthenes, 96
Thompson, C. B., 5
Thorndike, E. L., 113
Thought disorder, 96
Transituational community, 103
Trice, John, 11
Tricyclics, 97
Trifluoperazine, 96

U

Ulrich, Roger, 111
United Kingdom, 9, 102, 103
United States, 74, 89, 102, 103, 106
U. S. v. Chisholm, 41

V

Violence, 11
Virginia Colonies, 85
von Bertalanffy, L., 125

W

Walnut Street Jail, 88
Walsh, M. J., 100
Warner, A., 98-99
Watson, K. A., 11
Watzlawick, Paul, 123
Wetzel, R. J., 112
Wiersma, D., 7
Williams, P., 122

Wolf, M. M., 112, 115
Wooten, Barbara, 14
World War II, 102-103

Y

Yale University, 75
Youth
    institutions, 86